morale matters

morale matters

THE JOY OF REVEALING INNOCENCE,
EMPOWERMENT, AND SACRED WORK
IN PERSONAL MYTHOLOGY

VIOLETTA JEAN

LA MAISON DES RÊVES
PUBLISHING

COPYRIGHT © 2023 VIOLETTA JEAN

All rights reserved.

MORALE MATTERS
The Joy of Revealing Innocence, Empowerment, and Sacred Work in Personal Mythology

ISBN 978-1-5445-3867-9 *Hardcover*
       978-1-5445-3866-2 *Paperback*
       978-1-5445-3865-5 *Ebook*

For my trio of Angels
I call you mine, but I am yours forevermore.

Mama

contents

Prologue ix

SECTION I: MORALE MATTERS 1

SECTION II: ILLUMINATING PERSONAL MYTHOLOGY 15

SECTION III: RECLAIMING INNOCENCE 103

SECTION IV: BECOMING EMPOWERED 155

SECTION V: ENGAGING IN SACRED WORK 215

SECTION VI: MORALE OF A SONGBIRD - THE ALBUM 237

Epilogue 291

Acknowledgments 295

About the author 299

Notes 301

prologue

THIS BOOK WAS BORN FROM MY OWN STRUGGLES WITH morale.

When I first began the inward journey to find the source of morale, I was in a chronic state of overwhelm, without connection to my deeper, spiritual self. Physically, mentally, and emotionally, I was exhausted. I felt like I was always struggling to keep my head above water. My focus was nearly always on the hectic surface of life, schedules, to-dos, and the endless minutiae of life.

Daily I felt unrelenting guilt that I was not who I wanted to be—I was never productive, patient, kind, grateful, or loving enough. There was little cheer in my days. I didn't feel confident, empowered, or engaged with life in a fulfilling way. Any dreams I had held for myself had long been abandoned; I only dreamed of catching up. I always felt like I was waiting for *something* to feel better...

Decades deep into personal development work, I had read a hundred books on spirituality, connection with the Divine, worthiness, and the joy of living. Yet most of the time I didn't feel any of those things. As a nurse, I knew that living in a chronic state of survival was depleting my vitality and harming my body. I knew I wanted to experience the faith, beauty, abundance, and joy of living within love. I simply still didn't know how.

Most of all, I wanted to be a patient and loving mother to my three children. As a mother I wanted to show and demonstrate to my children that life is beautiful. I wanted them to feel that they are worthy of love and all the sweetness in life. I wanted them to know that their precious lives and the gifts they have been divinely bestowed matter. I wanted them to experience the joy and sacredness of living in their everyday lives. I wanted to create a beautiful life for myself and my family—a life that *felt* worth living.

What I didn't know then was that my joy and faith were trapped in a prison of fear. I had to learn how to authentically release my dependence on guilt, stress, and overwhelm. I had gone as far as I could reading and consuming ideas about love; it was time to embody love. I was facing the great chasm between love and fear. Transferring fundamental trust to love when one has relied on fear is a scary process. It takes time and perseverance.

I have discovered that cultivating morale is a pragmatic way to gradually transfer trust from fear to love. With the joy and well-being of my family on the line, I devoted myself to learning how to cultivate morale. The work takes place on a daily basis, within the context of everyday life. Tending to morale is not separate from living. It is the process of living well.

I do not speak often of my family of origin, children, or husband within these pages. I believe we share a sacred contract with one another. Revealing the details of our intimate relationships in a public way does not feel right to me. They are the owners of their own stories.

Still, the love I hold for my own children remains the heart and soul of this book. To offer the lesson of loving themselves unconditionally, I had to be a living example of loving myself unconditionally. I have come to understand, unequivocally, that in order to give unconditional love, I need to receive unconditional love, to reside within love.

In these pages, I set forth the intention to allow the unconditional love I have for my children to speak through me. My goal was to create a container for unconditional love and the best wisdom I possess for making it through hard times.

Even when we know that life is a blessing beyond measure, we can be unable to *receive* this gift when we are locked in fear. We find ourselves eternally waiting until it is safe to stop striving and running. Safe to be still, unwrap the gift of life, and be fully present to the joy and beauty of life.

I first came to this work as a mother deeply concerned for her children. No one can deny the depth of suffering many people are enduring at this time. Overwhelm, confusion, loss of hope, and despair are natural reactions to the diverse and monumental challenges humanity currently faces. Despair is a natural response to living in a world facing great challenges without a clear path forward. This book was born of the question, *How can I prepare my children to hold on to the beauty and joy of living while they face difficult and uncertain times?*

Life is hard, brutally hard at times. There is a reason the *Odyssey* has served as perhaps the most enduring model of life for centuries. The hero/ine sets out to face unknown challenges, challenges s/he cannot be fully prepared to meet. What is stunning to realize is how much of this epic journey takes place within, alone.

No book can save you from pain or make you all powerful. This is the arena of life. Yet there is a golden lifeline that comes straight through the earthly veil and holds you when you can't tell up from down. A lifeline woven of divine truth, love, comfort, and inspiration. You only need to reach for it. This is the story of how I wove my own golden lifeline.

I wrote this book as I went through my own process of finding morale; the manuscript was my constant companion. I imagine the book in your hands as a bedside companion, there to remind you daily that your morale matters. I pray this book will guide, comfort, and inspire you on your own journey to find the source of your morale.

SECTION I
morale matters

Morale: cheerful, confident engagement with the sacred work of living.

NO TOPIC IS MORE IMPORTANT OR TIMELY THAN MORALE. Morale is at the heart of how we choose to live our lives. It determines whether we feel we are thriving or merely surviving. The choice to cultivate hearty morale is available to each of us.

Many of us today face difficult challenges. We are being called upon to work together in unprecedented ways to create peace and preserve the dignity of life on Earth. In order to move toward a more loving, secure, and abundant future, we must act with intention. This is equally true on both the personal and collective levels.

None of the challenges we face diminishes the value, meaning, and beauty of life. In fact, it is by honoring the sacredness of life that we can move toward solutions most efficiently and powerfully.

When times of great challenge or change are before us, we must decide how we will respond. If we simply react to challenges, we are always at the mercy of our circumstances. We will not cultivate the joy that is available to us. We will not recognize the great power that each of us possesses. Nor will we engage with life to our fullest capacity.

The word morale speaks of something intangible, found both within the individual and reflected and shared within the whole. It honors the presence of spirit. Throughout history, morale has held the energetic power and promise of victory over overwhelming challenges.

Within this book, the word morale is always used in a positive sense. As it refers to cheer, confidence, and engagement with the sacred work of living, morale is a good thing in whatever quantity it is present. I use the word despair to refer to absence or critically low levels of morale.

At the heart of apathy and despair on the individual level is the legitimate concern of being swallowed up by the needs of the world. How do we hold the awareness of large-scale suffering and retain our ability to cultivate beautiful and joyful lives? We need to understand that what is cultivated in our personal lives is vital for the prosperity of humanity. We need to be reassured that we do not need to give up our own joy, comfort, and peace to contribute meaningfully to the whole of humanity. The authentic thriving and empowerment of every individual contributes to all of humanity.

The choice to cultivate morale is not a dismissal of the challenges we face; it is the decision to face challenges from our most empowered state. It is the choice to honor the beauty and joy of living as we work. Finally, it is the decision to actively engage with creating and implementing the solutions we want to see.

Morale is at the heart of the dignity of life. In a state of high morale, we see both ourselves and life itself as valuable. We feel equal to the challenges that life presents to us. There is meaning in the work we do.

The more challenging and uncertain our circumstances, the more important it is to consciously tend to our morale. Each of us has to make a conscious choice to honor and cultivate morale or risk falling into despair. Fundamentally, we are choosing whether we will reside in love or in fear.

Morale is the real-time, sum-total expression of your state of being. It reflects the true supply of vigor, attention, and motivation available to you.

Being you can feel very different than it does right now. Change, release, empowerment, and healing are all entirely possible. Never think I am suggesting that you add more and more weight to your days. On the contrary, hearty morale will serve to lighten your load.

My definition of morale includes the word cheer. Cheerfulness implies an acceptance of the work at hand, infused with a sufficiently vigorous "why" to render the work meaningful. Our work—which is living our lives—becomes pleasant when we honor the value of what we are doing and we are fully present.

Cheer is not something you have to create; it is something you allow. Morale is about tapping into the energy of love and operating from that abundance. When we feel safe, we can relax, and the joy of living is revealed.

When we choose to do work that directly contributes to something we value, we experience fulfillment. This is true whether we are working on the level of physical safety and comfort or engaging in lofty goals.

In a state of alignment, we are energized by a greater cause and our core values. The energetic connection to the greater good provides a buoyancy to the spirit. This buoyancy lives in the rhythm of the day. It is the antidote to the heaviness and drudgery that we often carry.

CULTIVATING MORALE

Morale is frequently honored during times of great difficulty and uncertainty—times without a clear ending. In times such as these, we honor that life is passing while we are engaged in a difficult trial. We recognize that we must not only fight for what matters but also hold what matters dear in the process. The future is not known, so we don't feel we can afford to wait to live. Because we cannot know when the challenges will end, we know we cannot be wasteful with our precious resources.

Learning to value morale rests upon the choice to honor the sacredness of life. When individuals choose to honor their own morale, they are committing acts of self-love. They are recognizing that the quality of their experience of life matters. Furthermore, they are recognizing their own power and value by contributing to something greater than themselves. When a community collectively chooses to honor morale, it is honoring the sacredness of humanity and life itself.

Throughout this book, I present two broad strategies for cultivating morale. The first method is primarily imaginal in nature. Though based in imagination and story, this strategy is transformative and fundamental to the cultivation of morale. It involves harnessing the tremendous power of imagination by working with personal mythology.

Our mythology holds and defines our constructs of both self and reality. There is a crucial relationship between self and what we perceive we are a part of, our reality. These two constructs and the relationship between them are what generate the quality of our morale.

The second broad strategy of cultivating morale is grounded in the physical and emotional self. Here we focus on establishing comforting and inspiring routines and rituals. I will discuss in depth the daily practical methods for cultivating and sustaining hearty morale.

DESPAIR

Despair is the joyless state, where all hope and confidence are lost and you no longer engage with the sacred work of living.

The more important something is, the more important it is to guard against despair. Despair is a state of disempowerment. If you listen carefully, you often will hear the great challenge of doing important things perfectly as a reason to not do anything. To not do anything beyond engaging in the drama of how awful it all is.

I choose to personify love, fear, morale, and despair because we are in an intimate relationship with these states. Acquainting ourselves with the voice and perspective of each state of being helps us to cultivate our relationships with intention.

Empowerment sees where there is opportunity to act with clarity and intention. Empowerment accepts the scope and scale of what can be done and gets to work. For empowerment, honest assessment is only the first stage, the place where one must begin. For despair, honest assessment is the end. There is nothing to be done from a place of disempowerment. Despair and hopelessness are blind to all who are diligently working on solving the problems facing humanity. They forget how right action and clear, purposeful thought, even by degrees, can lead to radically different results. They forget how paradigm shifts can change everything on a dime. How we are indeed still writing the future today.

PERSONAL AND COLLECTIVE MORALE

Morale is often spoken of in the context of groups. We are familiar with discussing the morale of the troops or civilian morale. Morale exists within teams, hospitals, schools, police departments, and businesses. Identity, proximity, common vision, and cause can all create a "container" of individuals. Within this container, the energies of all the individuals blend and mix. These individuals are in an energetic relationship.

When this relationship is healthy and serves the group, we say morale is high. In this scenario, the morale of the group is strengthening, supporting, and boosting the morale of the individuals.

When the relationship among the members of a group is weakening or draining the whole, we say morale is low. During times of hardship or war, attending to the morale of the group has been a valid and efficient approach to simultaneously care for the morale of individuals.

Every individual within the group also is contributing to the morale of the whole. As with every relationship, there is give and take. Relationships are cyclical because energy is always moving and flowing.

On the community and global levels, morale honors the need to join together with others for a common cause and for the common good. Again, cultivating morale is about the effective and efficient use of essential resources. The power of the actions, words, and energy of others is recognized as being equal to one's own. Hysteria and judgment in the face of a crisis are seen for the tragic waste of life force that they are. Communication and mutual respect are valued for the essential assets they are when working together.

In hard times, the value of what stands to be lost calls for all people to bring forth the best, most steady versions of themselves. It is time to come together, each person carrying their own portion of morale as well as they are able. Offering and receiving the sustaining support of others when necessary to boost morale.

Most definitions of the word morale refer to "spirit." Morale historically has been a way that people of diverse beliefs can speak of the collective spirit or energy that exists in groups of people. People accept this spirit or energy as something almost tangible. Morale is something that can be seen and worked with—boosted.

Methods for boosting troop morale, for example, aim to generate faith and trust in a cause, leaders, and a plan of action. When a plan of action is seen as valid, confidence is boosted. When a cause or plan holds meaning for the individuals, engagement is seen as worthwhile. Trust in leaders is also a critical component of group morale. Individuals must feel they are making a significant contribution to something that has value. Implementing these methods while preserving the dignity of life through small comforts and rituals boosts morale.

The belief that life is worth living may be called into question during hard times. The criteria by which we define a well-lived, happy life may not always be present. Joy, a sense of achievement, and peace may be altogether absent for a time when we experience devastating loss, trauma, disappointment, or uncertainty. We may not always be able to reach for happiness, but we can always aim to cultivate morale. As long as we remember our innate worthiness and power, we can choose to honor the pain and suffering we are enduring while we seek whatever cheer and useful work is present in the day.

We cannot truly honor and protect the value of our own lives while we dismiss and devalue another's life. The value of life as a whole must be elevated to the level of the sacred. Why the sacred? Because if we do not raise the value of life to the level of unconditional love, we will spend eternity trying to prove what is already true and searching for what cannot be lost. The love of life itself must be rescued from the death grip of fear if we are to experience freedom, joy, and peace. Freedom, joy, and meaning are at the heart of morale.

GIFTS OF CHALLENGING TIMES

In challenging times, we learn to mobilize all of our resources for the cause of carrying on with life. We learn what is most precious to us in life and what we can let go of. We come to better understand the vast resources we can call upon, within and outside ourselves. In a state of high morale, we preserve as best we can the dignity and beauty of living life regardless of our circumstances.

In hard times, there is no point in denying the challenges we are facing, because they are clearly present and known. Yet when we look for it, the awe-inspiring beauty of ephemeral life is all the more clear to behold. Kindness, comfort, and inspiration shine forth like beacons in the darkest of times. We can choose to deeply ground ourselves in what truly matters to us. We can preserve and embody our most precious values with newfound clarity and intention. We begin to rely on what is authentic because its realness can be felt.

The essential balance between staying grounded and inspired must be cultivated. We innately know we cannot waste energy in the bipolar swings of mania and despair. Morale does not dismiss the hard emotions of fatigue, despair, hopelessness, anger, or mourning. It is morale's fundamental task to care for the self that struggles and suffers from these emotions.

DISCOVER THE SOURCE

A consideration of morale reflects a fundamental respect for and understanding of what it means to be human. When cultivating morale, we are concerned with the quality of life as much as survival. When we validate the importance of the quality of our own experiences, we validate that there is inherent meaning in *being human*, *being* alive. A high state of morale is defined by the presence of cheer, enthusiasm, and zest, not simply by what is accomplished. Therefore, the question becomes *what is the source of these emotions?* Equally important is *what is blocking these emotions?*

If you have suffered from low morale, you have likely turned to superficial pleasures to supply feelings of cheer, enthusiasm, and zest. Shopping, chemicals, food, sex, travel, and entertainment are some of the common ways we attempt to raise morale. Yet these alone will not generate a sense of true morale. It is noteworthy how overdependence on any of these sources of pleasure is detrimental to well-being. Each leads to some type of toxicity, such as debt, clutter, stress, or loss of physical vitality. The problem lies in that while we are focusing on temporary relief, we are neglecting fundamental needs.

We are composed of mind, body, and spirit. When the spirit is in need, we require spiritual solutions, not simply physical distractions. To experience a deep sense of morale, we have to engage with life from the whole self. We have to live from the full depths of ourselves—mind, body, and spirit. What does it mean to be living from mind, body, and spirit? It means honoring the voice, values, and needs of each of these aspects of self. When we learn to do this, we then gain access to the wisdom and resources that each aspect of self holds.

Morale exists squarely in linear time but can be supplied from sources beyond time and space. This truth is reflected in the natural inclination of humans to work with the mystery beyond physical reality. We work with this mystery through spiritual and religious practices. We can also work with the mystery through the arts and sciences.

Living according to morale does not mean living a small life. Humans are capable of achieving extraordinary things by honoring morale. Authentic joy and confidence in one's work establishes a virtuous cycle. The work is feeding morale, and morale is fueling the work.

No one can be expected to always remain in a state of high morale. When and where you can muster your daily resolve, please do. It will serve not only you but also all of those around you. When the time comes that, for whatever reason, you seem unable to muster the resources of your mind, body, and spirit, take heart. When we are tired, restless, irritable, anxious, sad, frustrated, angry, or grieving, adding guilt only makes regaining morale more difficult.

You are always worthy of exquisite self-care. Our state of morale must never be used to measure or establish our worthiness. Monitoring morale is a tool for care of self, never a weapon against self.

During times of low morale, rest when and where you can. I pray those around you will carry morale until you are renewed. In the meantime, drink deeply from the beauty of nature. Savor the comforting reassurance of personal self-care rituals. Receive whatever love, support, and encouragement are available to you. Give yourself time and space. Engage with life in whatever small ways you can—even if they seem to be insignificant. Take the time you need to genuinely restore your morale.

The source of morale will never be found in fear. Fear takes, whereas love supplies. Fear takes because it is consuming our focus, attention, time, and energy without giving anything back. Love can be seen as the energy that creates, whereas fear is a void. Seeking to control and manipulate what one can is natural, but this can become an exercise in draining drama when what is required is steady resolve, commitment, and patience.

In order to cultivate morale, we must remain connected to the heart of what we are living and fighting for. If we lose focus, despair says, "What is the point? Look how awful it all is! It's all so far gone. Can't you see? Don't be a fool. It's hopeless."

In a state of high morale, we look out into the beauty of the world, see the myriad souls, and are filled with love, respect, and resolve. We know there is work to be done and get to the all-important questions: *What do I wish to experience and create in the world? What is within my power to do now?* The answers to these questions lie within your personal mythology.

SECTION II
illuminating personal mythology

THE GREAT DRAMA BETWEEN LOVE AND FEAR TAKES PLACE within the story of your own personal mythology. Your work must begin with you.

Personal: of or relating to a particular person; private, individual.

—MERRIAM-WEBSTER

Mythology: an allegorical narrative.

—MERRIAM-WEBSTER

Allegory: a story, play, poem, picture, or other work in which the characters and events represent particular qualities or ideas that relate to morals, religion, or politics.

—CAMBRIDGE DICTIONARY

Each of us resides within a multidimensional story composed of words, images, biology, scent, sound, taste, touch, and memory. Your story contains all the defining events of your life and holds your essential relationships. Even more critically, your personal mythology (the allegorical narrative of your life) assigns meaning to all these events and relationships. Your mythology contains your best understanding of the hero/ine—the essential self—as well as everything outside yourself. It defines the world as you personally have come to know it and defines your place within it. In short, your personal mythology holds together everything that has meaning for you in a coherent body.

THE STORY OF YOU AND THE WORLD

Every word of every line of your personal mythology holds energy. It is the energy of you.

The relationship between the personal world of self and the outer world as you understand it is the source of your morale. Morale reflects how cheerful, confident, and engaged you feel based on your own understanding of the relationship between your self and the world.

Personal mythology is a container. It contains facts, imagination, and a functional system of personal logic based upon our beliefs. We use the logic born of our own understanding to make all of our decisions. When we talk about beliefs, this is what we are referring to, but mythology is so much more. In a very real way, our personal mythology is our energetic home. We carry it with us everywhere we go.

We are constantly making sense of all we experience or want to experience through the lens of this story. If something is not written into our personal mythologies, we will not feel or act as if that thing exists. Even though joy and abundance are our natural states, we are able to separate ourselves from these resources through a fearful story. If pleasure, joy, and happiness are written as rewards, then we will find ourselves always waiting to feel worthy of them. Sometimes, tragically, these rewards are written only into the afterlife.

Re-creating a personal mythology within which one's morale can thrive is not a simple thing. Many of the foundational laws and structures of our mythologies were placed before we were aware there was a choice in how we see reality and ourselves. Once these concepts have been accepted as reality and assimilated into our identities, seeing, evaluating, and re-creating them requires focus, time, and intention.

The marriage between imagination and the facts of the physical world, between the Divine and the earthly, is the fertile ground of personal mythology. A state of empowerment is basically the ability to discern fact from fiction and use imagination to one's own benefit.

Your personal mythology is the story unique to you that answers all the ultimate questions of life and defines your place in the world. Sources of inspiration for your personal mythology are more varied now than at any other time in human history. We gather imagery and wisdom from our families of origin, culture, religion, education, books, myths, movies, art, and music.

Other vital sources of mythology are the news and media. Modern news poses several unique challenges for individuals trying to find their places in the world. Global news, in particular, has expanded the scope of the individual's world. It has thereby altered the perception of the individual's power in relation to the whole. In a bigger world, our innate value and contribution can feel less significant.

Furthermore, the speed with which we are aware of changes in the world creates instability in our understanding of the world. The impact of the combined changes of scope and stability on our sense of empowerment have enormous implications on morale. This is true even if we feel global events do not affect us personally. Just as our own morale feeds into the morale of humanity, the morale of humanity informs our own.

We have not yet found our bearing as individuals in the context of an expanding worldview. In order to effectively cultivate morale, we need to connect our personal lives and actions to our understanding of the world in a meaningful way. In order to experience *sustainable* morale, we have to find a way to engage and contribute within the scope of an individual life. If we fail to establish essential personal scope, we experience overwhelm and eventually despair.

In modern times, we are able to blend mythologies from the East, West, North, and South. We now have access to wisdom, imagery, philosophy, science, and art across the time span of human history. While sources of personal mythology have always varied, in the past a person's mythology typically was tied to a cohesive and formalized body of myths. This body of myths served to answer all of the person's ultimate questions.

Formal religions are among the most common and enduring containers for understanding the self within a worldview. In the case of religion and isolated cultures, worldview was shared and reinforced by a community of like-minded individuals. As cultures have mixed and evolved, belief in a single worldview has largely broken down.

People now have much greater freedom in how they decide to see themselves and the world. Yet many people are struggling tremendously with an insufficient worldview—struggling to find a mythology that is grand enough to hold all the beauty, joy, pain, and suffering they see and experience in a meaningful and self-sustaining way.

Everywhere you turn you find five bullet remedies for whatever ails you. I believe we are seeking a return to depth. Not covering the reality of our mortality or the ever-present, deep mystery within which we all live. There is no one size fits all solution for human suffering. We have to be willing to reflect on the great existential questions to connect to our true depths.

How do we manage the reality that we are all vulnerable? At any moment we can lose all that we care most deeply about. What is worth building our lives upon? What would we be unwilling to put down, even in the face of death?

Personal mythology is essentially the energetic home you have created for your essential self here on Earth. The purpose of exploring personal mythology is to help you declutter and reimagine your mythology so that it can house the full potential, power, joy, and magnificence of your essential self.

ULTIMATE QUESTIONS

The creative potential for designing your own personal mythology is limitless, but to harness this power, you must cultivate intention. First, you have to come to know your current mythology and gain an understanding of how all the pieces you have used work together. An efficient method for doing this is to reflect upon your own answers to the ultimate questions below. The answers to these questions are encoded in our beliefs.

When I first started to recognize the power of beliefs, I began the work of identifying and releasing surface limiting beliefs one by one. Looking back, I can see how inefficient this method was. My approach was quite random and, therefore, ineffective.

Beliefs we are unaware of can be tangled up in decades of self-manipulation and denial. The beliefs we are aware of are often tied to much deeper, ancient beliefs in our personal timelines. If these core, ancient beliefs are painful, they are covered in decades of defense, denial, and protection.

Throughout the pages of this book, I reveal all of my own answers to the ultimate questions. The clarity of being I have gained from seeking to understand and intentionally choosing my own answers has been transformational. I reveal my answers to illustrate the process of exploring personal mythology, not to answer the ultimate questions for you.

Your answers to the ultimate questions may change over time, but begin with getting to know your current best answers. You will know you have revealed your true beliefs to yourself when the answers explain your actual experience of yourself and life.

As you work on the following journal prompt, reflect on the sources of your answers and whether or not you would choose to hold each belief. Uncovering your authentic beliefs will take time and courage, especially if you do not wish to live according to these answers.

You will benefit from the clarity of being that understanding your personal mythology brings. Your answer to each of the following questions has a direct bearing on your personal morale. Reflecting on all the ultimate questions as a whole will help you become intimate with your own personal mythology.

journaling prompt

Take time to contemplate, meditate, and journal about each of these questions. Go as deeply as you would like with this exercise. If any question feels overwhelming or your current answer is painful, be gentle with yourself. There is no hurry to unravel your personal mythology. Furthermore, there will always be room for mystery. You get to decide for yourself. There is no response that is more true or valid than your own authentic answers. I only encourage awareness and choosing with intention for yourself.

1. How did the world come to be?

2. What is the meaning of life?

3. How do I relate with the mystery—that which I do not understand?

4. What should I do?

5. What is love?

6. What is the meaning of suffering?

7. What's valuable?

8. How am I of value?

9. How do I become whole?

10. What is within my power?

11. How do I relate to that which is outside of my power?

12. How can I be safe?

13. How can I keep my loved ones safe?

14. How do I relate to others?

15. What happens when I die?

Ultimate questions are called questions for a reason. We are each living out the answers to these questions. What questions are you currently seeking to answer in your life? What are the truest, most complete answers you have at this point in your life? When you look at these questions, you may fail to recognize that you do, in fact, possess beliefs that serve to answer them—even if you believe the answers are unknowable.

The beliefs we hold that answer the ultimate questions are powerful, whether or not they are readily retrievable. If you have not meditated on the questions with intention, your answers are likely completely by default. It is also possible that some of your own beliefs conflict with one another. For example, you may believe that love is the most powerful force yet also believe that acting from fear will keep you safest.

Do your answers to these questions bring clarity around how you feel about life? About yourself? The combined answers to these questions reveal the most fundamental assumptions and essential relationships embedded in your belief systems. Understanding your beliefs around the ultimate questions illuminates the most critical structure of your personal mythology. Your personal internal logic is founded in these beliefs.

If we consider ourselves to be a valuable part of something bigger than ourselves that also holds value, we will likely experience high morale. If we believe neither ourselves nor the outer world holds value, then we will inevitably suffer from low morale. Thankfully, there are elements, or strands, of morale that can be identified and strengthened with intention.

Thomas Merton said, "The greatest need of our time is to clean out the enormous mass of mental and emotional rubbish that clutters our minds." If we have been distracted or unaware of the greater questions of life, we likely have not taken care to examine, understand, or curate our beliefs about ourselves and reality.

As we turn into our vast inner worlds, we begin to explore our stories, our mythologies. We begin to ask, *Who am I, and what power and resources do I possess? What am I a part of, and how do I fit into it?* We may have taken our personal mythologies for granted all of our lives, but there are two times when we turn our attention to the stories we are living within:

- When events cause significant disruption to our understanding of self and the world

- When we explore our own mythologies with intention to purposefully rewrite them

In either situation, we can gain a better understanding of the many assumptions we have been operating within.

Our mythologies have been forming since before we were conscious enough to question them. Generally, we simply accept the narratives we have been given about ourselves and the world. Details of our mythologies are stored in both our conscious and subconscious minds. These stories weave together the fabric of our own realities.

If we believe our innocence has been lost, we will not recognize our everlasting worthiness. When we are not self-possessed of mind, body, and spirit, we will not believe we are as powerful as we truly are. If we have built our personal mythologies within the fear paradigm that is most prevalent in the world today, we will further harm and disempower ourselves through guilt, blame, and judgment.

If, however, we have built our personal mythologies within the paradigm of love, we will have access to comfort, worthiness, beauty, and joy, even through the hardest of times.

SPIRITUAL PRAGMATISM

At this point on my personal journey, I have become what I call a spiritual pragmatist. For example, I would not spend time or energy pondering the question of whether or not there can be true altruism. The fact that humans feel good when doing what they believe to be good is beautiful, full stop. This human is generating good, internally in the presence of good, and expressing good. I do not see value in exploring the question of whether this alignment is somehow deeply self-centered. I consider this mental exercise to be walking right off the edge of human meaning.

I share this example to provide a tone and a scope for this work. I consider a concept or image meaningful in a human sense if it can hold and move energy. Then it is a question of how the energy is experienced and whether or not it moves an individual toward love or fear. I am interested in how I can most effectively align the sum total of my being with my core values.

As a pragmatist, I'm not interested in deconstructing reality to the point it is no longer a relevant container for human life. I wish to provide reliable and practical comfort, today, for anyone who might be in need of it. I believe there are universal, timeless, practical, spiritual truths. Truths that can be assembled and constructed in a solid and systematic way to provide shelter in any storm and a place to heal.

GOD

Webster's first entry of God is as follows.

God: the supreme or ultimate reality.

This bare definition is a wonderful starting point for a meaningful discussion of God. What is the reality that lies beneath our sensory perceptions and sense of self? What is the original and final reality, beneath and beyond space and time? What is our relationship to this divine mystery?

I imagine that every individual's understanding and experience of God is as unique as the individual. However, Webster's simple definition of God can be used to communicate a universal experience of being part of something that is greater than ourselves.

For many, stripping away the baggage that the word God carries for them may be quite beneficial—allowing them to look with fresh eyes at the great questions of life. For others, the word or concept of God may be absent altogether; yet, in its absence, it remains a force as powerful as an absent parent. For some, the word God is the most beautiful and important concept in reality. For others still, the essence of ultimate reality may be captured in an alternative word, such as universe. Whichever the case, there is a relationship that is paramount in our experience of life. How do we relate to the mystery beyond our own understanding?

Awareness and Presence

Life is the joy and sorrow of God expressing self in intimate form.

What is God if not presence and awareness?

Divine presence is real, simultaneously universal and intimate. Just like gravity, it can be relied upon to support, comfort, and guide you. It is this presence that we seek in the faces of our loved ones and in the beauty of nature. Think of the creative intelligence encoded within a humble sunflower seed or the DNA of a baby. The omnipresence of the Divine is so incredibly obvious that it can be completely overlooked.

I find there is so much evidence for God's joy and delight in the intimate and personal. Being able to witness and share in the great beauty and great sorrow of God in intimate form is a tremendous blessing. When we honor this experience, we are actually loving God within ourselves and in others. Being in touch with this truth is the ultimate source of joie de vivre (exuberant enjoyment of life) and courage. From the state of wholeness, our natural inclination is to nurture and respond to the suffering of others with compassion and care.

The way we characterize God, or the mystery, determines whether our relationship to life is trusting, defensive, or hostile. This same fundamental question exists within ourselves as well. *Is our own nature to be trusted or fought against?* Understanding and working with fundamental beliefs is the most efficient way to answer these questions with intention. The decision to embrace the most loving beliefs that feel authentic to you results in a powerful boost in morale.

It has been my experience that trusting in ever more loving beliefs becomes a virtuous cycle. As we release fearful beliefs, we simply feel better. Consequently, our relationships to self and others improve. We experience greater mental, emotional, and physical health. This is because physically, mentally, emotionally, and spiritually we are designed to live from love. We thrive when we align with loving beliefs because we *are* love.

HYGGE AND THE DIVINE VEIL OF INTIMACY

According to Wikipedia, "the word *hygge* comes from a Danish word meaning 'to give courage, comfort, joy.' *Hygge* stems from *hyggja* which means 'to think' in Old Norse. *Hygge* is built from the Old Norse word *hugr* which later became the hug which means the soul, mind, consciousness."

In *The Book of Hygge* by Louisa Thomsen Brits, she explains,

> An essential ingredient to hygge is the boundary that marks a place or delineates a moment—a fence, a circle of cushions, or a stolen half hour. The boundaries that we put in place when we hygger can be both physical and temporal—setting aside an hour to visit a friend, pulling chairs into a circle around a campfire, or closing the door to secure a den to watch a film in peace. When we arrange office furniture, decide where to sit on a bus, or set out a picnic rug, we establish a boundary and a point of focus and make space for the spirit of hygge to breathe life and warmth into our activities. When we establish limits, we can relax and dwell in a place or moment. Our dreams, thoughts, and conversations can unfurl in peace. We find ourselves in a place where we can believe that good things will happen.

I believe all of life is divine hygge. What if the apparent separation of God into individual atoms, cells, and souls is a result of the divine desire for intimacy? What if life is born of the desire to behold and be held? Science is beginning to reveal the reality of the fabric of life truly being one. Mystics, philosophers, and religious practitioners espoused this beautiful idea long before it was revealed by science.

If all is one, then we are truly one in God. We are all facets or tiny faces of God. The fabric of reality is in constant movement, from the electrons in atoms to the planets around stars, because it is all living. Everything is composed of divine intelligence and energy.

Creation, play, discovery, language, music, romance, and family as we experience them all rely upon the apparent separation of the whole into functional, creative units.

When caring for and recognizing the sacred in both self and others, we are serving God. From this perspective, we receive when we give and give when we receive. I cannot imagine a more eternally morale-boosting belief than this. Supreme worthiness, value, and beauty are written into everything we are and experience. The more we are able to draw ourselves within the circle of the Divine, the more sacred life will feel.

The question becomes, how do we connect this grand idea into our daily lives? How do we carry the truth of oneness into a world that is suffering so dearly due to a sense of separation? We are each born with the survival instinct to protect the self and those we love. Each of us possesses a mind that is constantly judging and evaluating our environments in relation to the self.

Understandably, the pain of separation leads many to want to transcend the human experience altogether. Yet life is not a problem to be solved or a condition we need to be saved from. Engaging with life is our sacred work.

The soul is deeply in love with human life. The soul loves to be part of the beauty and love of the Divine dancing with earthly life.

What if God enjoys our blossoming and unfolding as a gardener revels in the full cycle of the flower? What if all that is unfolding in time and space is sacred?

The majesty of the seasons changing before our eyes is a reminder that we are part of something grand and beautiful, filling our hearts with awe and wonder. Life is full of intimate details and sweeping strokes of inexpressible beauty. We are nurtured and sustained by it. And yet we innately know the other side of intimacy is loss. A great deal of personal mythology is designed around coping with this truth.

We long to escape, bury, hide, and deny our vulnerability. Without a framework beyond the shallow surface of daily life to hold us, we do not have the courage to face loss. Every day we hear stories of tremendous pain and suffering. We respond by wanting to separate ourselves from others and suffering, but this is a vicious cycle born of fear.

The way I see it, we are not here on Earth to pretend we don't see it. We are not meant to endlessly fight or wait quietly for life to pass. We are meant to experience our humanness deeply. We are made to hold all of it, the beauty, joy, and pain. The courage, resilience, and confidence from this belief alone is transformational.

NOBLE CELL, NOBLE SELF

The primordial cell represents the birth of the personal. A space separated, a first divine breath, where God began to experience divine self in a new way—a rich, intimate, living way. Over time, colors, sounds, tastes, and touch filled the awareness of self and a brilliant veil fell from the heavens. A veil born from the unique experience of living with the constant input of our senses. The veil created the sense of time and space. As humans with the holy gift of imagination, we can throw innumerable sounds, images, tastes, and feelings on the veil as we experience ourselves in the world.

Humanity is meant to explore and experience life, the grand beauty and the grand suffering. Yet, when we go deep enough within or far enough without, we find the eternal Divine. Beyond the veil, the fullness and completeness of the Divine still reigns supreme.

Perhaps divine hygge began with the smallest unit of life, the cell. The cell provides a beautiful metaphor for the self. Firstly, the cell maintains a cell wall. This wall encircles a space that is itself and simultaneously defines not-self. This division is the birth of intimacy and intention.

While I cannot predict what state of being you are currently in or what challenges you face, I believe there is great solace and pragmatic guidance in remembering that you are a living entity. There are known universal principles that govern all of life.

As a living entity, the cell does not simply react to all that it encounters. It is not purely at the mercy of its environment. The cell wall allows the cell to be selective as to what it brings into its internal environment. The cell wall allows the cell to create with intention its own internal conditions or homeostasis.

Excerpt from *Human Anatomy & Physiology*, Fourth Edition, by Elaine N. Marieb:

> Walter Cannon, an American physiologist of the early twentieth century, spoke of the "wisdom of the body," and he coined the word homeostasis to describe its ability to maintain relatively stable internal conditions even though the outside world changes continuously. Although the literal translation of homeostasis is "unchanging," the term does not really mean a static, or unchanging, state. Rather, it indicates a dynamic state of equilibrium, or balance, in which internal conditions vary, but always within relatively narrow limits.

The cell wall must provide an exchange with the environment. Openness and exchange are written into the very design of life. The cell never arrives "there," a fixed state. To be alive is to be in a state of movement. Life requires constant assessment and feedback followed by response.

Homeostasis is essentially the morale of the cell. The cell is able to fully engage with life as it was designed when its own internal needs are attended to. The cell naturally seeks what is most nurturing from its environment and aims to keep out that which is harmful. It releases the inevitable waste that accumulates as a result of living processes, or it suffers the consequence of toxic buildup. Cells also possess the ability to move. The cell moves away from that which is harmful and moves toward nurturing conditions, away from pain and toward pleasure.

A study of the noble cell reveals the most basic definition of life and its implications. The requirements of a thriving state for a cell are fundamentally no different than for you or me.

In essence, the metaphor of the cell strips life down to its most fundamental elements. It allows us to see, without judgment, an eternal framework for how to live well. The distance and ability to regard the cell as an objective whole offer a unique perspective on the living being. Who are we to judge or define the purpose of a cell? The cell is what it is in scale, and it aims to live in alignment with the conditions necessary for its survival and thriving. Objective distance allows for the development of a deep respect for the beauty of what simply is.

The beauty of this basic framework of life is how seamlessly it applies to any "living" system: the self, belief systems, relationships, homes, organizations, countries, and, ultimately, Mother Earth herself. Life requires scope, balance, methods for receiving life-sustaining nutrients, and a process for eliminating waste from life processes. There must be freedom to move toward what is beneficial and away from that which is harmful. The "living" entity by definition is also always in a state of movement. It must exert energy in maintaining a state of homeostasis. Stillness, or a perfectly stable state, is synonymous with death.

THE KINGDOM OF THE ESSENTIAL SELF

You are a domain, a kingdom, a vessel. There is a functional circle that contains your essential self.

For many, the royal archetype is extraordinarily powerful. The imagery of the kingdom calls to mind an expansive, abundant realm where we are truly at home. We experience a deep sense of belonging and empowerment when we reside within our interior kingdom.

We have within our own realm an abundance of all that we could ever need. The archetypal king or queen possesses innate worthiness and authentic power that is granted as a birthright. A thriving king or queen is a force for good. They do not feel a need to compete or take from another. The important thing to remember is that every man, woman, and child is a kingdom. By showing up in our own dignity, we call to the nobility within others.

Whether you embrace your power or not, you are always the ultimate ruler of your kingdom. It is a power you are born into, and it simply cannot be taken away. We do, however, need to learn to wield our own power with intention.

Invitation to the Full Essential Self

The essential self is composed of multiple entities that dance within and outside of time and space. There are many useful models to describe the nature and relationship of these interior entities.

Religion, philosophy, and psychology have all described the multidimensionality of the interior self. As is true with all words, the meaning and energy contained within these terms is personal. It is up to each of us to come to know and understand our full essential self.

I devised the following diagram to portray my own understanding of the full essential self. I do not claim that it is right or perfect, but it is a framework that supports me and my morale. It gives me an idea of both where suffering may be coming from and how to potentially address it. I hope it will serve to inspire and stimulate your own understanding of the full self.

The fundamental question that led me to view the essential self in this way was, *What is the relationship between the realms of the Divine and humanity? How do the universal and personal relate to one another?* The areas of overlap that make up the ego, the soul, and the higher self can be viewed as bayous. This is where earthly and divine energies commingle—much like the varied channels of the cell wall, designed to allow for selective communication and exchange of nutrients and information and the release of wastes. Again, even from the beginning, on the cellular level, life requires movement, exchange, and openness.

When we truly become aware and open to these varied aspects of ourselves, we realize there is as much intimacy within us as without. In its own right, interior life is a vastly important dimension of life as human beings.

ANATOMY OF THE FULL ESSENTIAL SELF

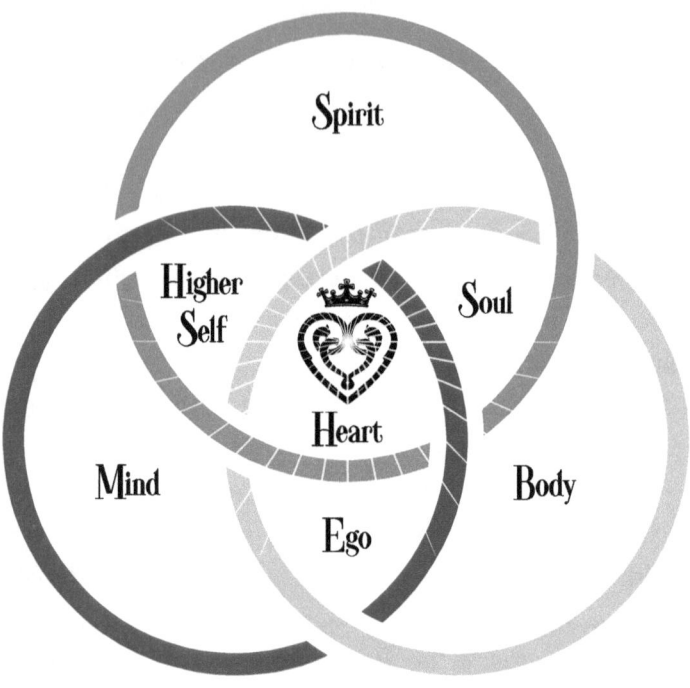

NAME	DESCRIPTION	GIFTS
Spirit	Divine Differentiated Energy	Vitality and Awe
Mind	Divine Differentiated Consciousness	Awareness, Focus, and Imagination
Body	Alchemical Container	Intimacy of Life
Ego	Personal Consciousness—Rooted in Physical Reality	Earthly Safety and Identity
Higher Self	Personal Consciousness—Connected to Divine	Core Values and Purpose
Soul	Divine Intimacy—Connected to Physical Reality	Joie de Vivre and Passion
Heart	Wholeness of Self—Meeting Place of All Aspects of Self	Compass and Morale—Vital Sign of the Full Essential Self

I do not choose to believe in a hierarchy among the aspects of self. My fundamental goal is to understand and bring harmony to the whole. When we focus too much on the higher self, we risk losing a sense of groundedness in our lives. Likewise, when we focus too much on the soul, we risk missing the inspiration and awe that the higher self provides. When we are able to embody the full essential self, we experience wholeness. We are able to access and hold more of the joy, peace, beauty, energy, abundance, pleasure, awe, and wonder that life offers.

The whole self is worthy of love. You do not have to reject or judge thoughts, feelings, or natural desires to be worthy or acceptable. Love seeks to understand. All voices within the self can be safely welcomed and heard. I do not believe that we must engage in a lifelong battle against any part of us. For example, I have found that having a clear understanding of and open communication between my ego and higher self is more beneficial than living in a state of conflict.

All aspects of the essential self are constantly communicating with us. Some people lead more from the mental aspect of the self while others lead more from the physical or spiritual. However, to be whole, we must provide a safe space for all aspects of the self to communicate. Wherever we do not have safety, we cannot have pure honesty. When we don't have self-honesty, we are not fully empowered.

To be self-possessed is to honor and embody the full self. All the parts composing the essential self have been designed with intention and intelligence. Each component of self is valuable. Each component has its own recognizable energy and represents a unique perspective. Each part of self holds invaluable resources.

Your personal mythology dictates the parts of yourself you will acknowledge, respect, and listen to. In a very real sense, personal mythology ties together the energy of the divine universal and the interior, intimate world of the essential self. You have to write yourself into full being.

If your spirit, soul, higher self, ego, body, or heart is not given meaning and voice within your personal mythology, you will not have access to it. All the aspects of the full essential self are always there, but we have to invite them into our awareness to experience them intimately. If an aspect of the essential is not acknowledged or honored, lack of harmony will lead to symptoms.

Spirit

For the purpose of this discussion, the spirit is differentiated divine energy. The spirit holds reserves of boundless energy for the essential self. God, the Divine, light, and love are all essentially synonyms for the spirit. The energy of the spirit is alive. It is love.

Our personal energy comes from much, much more than the intake of physical calories. We all know and have experienced the dramatic highs and lows of energy related to art, news, and events. Sometimes we experience these highs and lows and are not even able to identify the source.

Great and sudden waves of energy reveal the presence of the spirit in self. Personal mythology is the container of personal, differentiated spiritual energy. Beliefs block or allow the flow of boundless spiritual energy through the self.

Mind

Deep within the magical show of time and space is where our deepest consciousness dwells. Ultimately, the mind is the source of awareness and focus. The mind is divine differentiated consciousness.

The mind is a creative instrument. It is far more than a processor of information and data. It is more than a storage container of memories. The mind is the source of imagination and extraordinary creative power in both the inner and outer worlds.

Within the body is the physical brain, which processes sensory input and experiences the veil as reality. We are aware of far more going on within our conscious mind than the processing of this data, however. We are aware of the ego, the narrator, constantly evaluating and judging our experiences. We also are able to dream things that have never been and play with memory like words of poetry. Even when in the midst of sensory input from the exterior world, an interior world that retains independence remains. This presence of mind is beyond time and space and is evidence that our essential self is connected to and capable of creating from infinite abundance. There was a time in the development of philosophy when this truth was discussed without resistance. Humans were invited to explore this realm of knowledge and wisdom and harvest its great resources.

Body

The body can be seen as the alchemical container of a divine being incarnate in time and space. It allows for intimacy of experience and sacred evolution. The body is our original soulmate. It is a divine gift and an essential part of the physical experience of human life.

The physical body is always in communication with the rest of the essential self. The experience of our own energy in motion—emotion—is felt in the body. The chakra centers are located within the physical body and energetically connect the body to the other aspects of self. We must honor and respect our physical self in order to fully receive the messages and resources of the full essential self.

Ego

The ego is the aspect of self we are most familiar with. The voice of the ego is clear, and it accompanies us throughout our days. The ego can be thought of as the narrator of our personal mythology.

I have tremendous compassion for the ego, which has been assigned a very hard task. With extremely limited understanding and resources, the ego attempts to keep us safe in the physical world. Ever on the lookout for danger, the ego finds threats everywhere. It serves to protect us from physical, emotional, social, and psychological pain.

I believe the ego is a voice that is inseparable from the human experience—it serves a purpose and is part of our divine design. Therefore, I choose to honor and respect my ego. I treat her with patience, kindness, and love. I place my ego within the loving care of my full essential self.

The ego is fundamentally concerned with safety and therefore wants assurance that physical and social needs will be met. Taking care of these needs frees us to turn our attention to higher-level pursuits. When we attempt to achieve higher-level goals while ignoring the needs of the ego, we create unnecessary drama and suffering.

The ego is like the baby who cries out in need of food or comfort or coos contentedly when her needs are met. When the baby is crying, we may carry on trying to do all the things, ignoring her cries. We imagine she will be comforted when the interminable list is done—when *enough* is done.

Stop. Feed the baby and comfort her. The madness will calm, and you can once again move with grace and presence. Don't worry that the baby's needs will overwhelm you. You can take care of the baby. Hold the baby in love. Assure the baby she is safe, her needs matter, and you are there.

There is no substitute for love, attention, and honoring the fundamental needs of the baby. No rattle will calm a hungry baby for long. The baby is naturally joyful and content when her needs are met. Routines and rituals can comfort the baby and provide a genuine sense of security and well-being. Speak lovingly to the baby, especially when she is afraid or distressed. You cannot rationalize away the needs of the baby or judge the baby's needs. They simply are, and they must be accepted.

The idea of rejecting the ego is actually a bit ironic because the ego is the aspect of self that rejects. The ego is willing to hurt, demean, and reject the self when it feels safety is on the line. The ego is even willing to hurt and reject itself because it believes tying up our own energy in fear keeps us contracted and, therefore, safe.

When the ego tries to hold the complexity, beauty, and power of the full essential self, it is understandably overwhelmed. The ego knows it is not equal to controlling or understanding the full essential self.

No book or program can teach the ego how to successfully run this show. The ego does not have access to the full design of life or our infinite resources. Only the full essential self operates from this vantage point.

Higher Self

The higher self is the interface between the spirit and the mind. It retains the holy impulse of love to continuously evolve and grow.

The higher self holds our individual core values, and it is the seat of conscience. The higher self is constantly aware of the gap between our core values and our real expression at any given time. This gap is the source of great suffering for us, and I will return to this topic later. For now, suffice it to say that even though we receive and transmute the energy of the sun's rays, we were never intended to be one with the sun. Pure, constant, unfailing expression of ideals is not what the human experience is about. We are alchemical. I believe we are creating gold, but perfection is not our way.

The higher self has a clear, peaceful, and loving way of communicating. I have come to recognize a distinctness of sound or sparkle about a phrase, image, or story when my higher self is speaking to me. I know that I will be able to recall when and where I first heard an idea that is highlighted in this way. I almost hear, "This is for you." Even decades later, I recall the messages that I now recognize as guideposts from my higher self.

Soul

"It is only through mystery and madness that the soul is revealed."

—THOMAS MOORE

I will forever be grateful for the separation of soul from spirit as defined by Thomas Moore in *Care of the Soul*. "Not a thing but a quality or dimension of experiencing life and ourselves. It has to do with depth, value, relatedness, heart and personal substance."

At the time I was guided to this book, I held the values of the higher self above all else. Through the lens of unworthiness, the pursuit of my higher values resembled a quest for perfection. Though my soul was communicating with me through a deep sense of sadness, longing, and desire to feel grounded, I did not recognize the source of my suffering. I kept pushing harder for worthiness through purity. In *Care of the Soul*, Thomas Moore gave meaning and value to the voice of my soul.

In my own understanding, the soul is the rich, physical, earthly aspect of the Divine embodied in the physical. The soul is the means by which God experiences the richness of intimacy. It is nourished by colors, textures, flavors, emotions, and beauty that can be experienced by the Divine only through physical life.

The soul is willing to experience the pain of separation to feel the ecstasy of union and finds as much valuable life carried in loss as presence—in reaching as arriving. All of the uncertainty behind most of our anxiety and fear is rich, fertile ground for the soul because it is a part of life. The soul is not afraid. It is absolutely, head over heels in love with earthly life. All of it. Come what may. The soul is the source of joie de vivre.

We have to write the value and perspective of the soul into our personal mythologies and into our every day to receive its gifts. This takes courage because the soul knows that exquisite vulnerability and risk are a necessary part of living a beautiful life. The soul wants to live in the singular beauty that is your life, your passions, and your essence, and it calls you to hygge in your one and only fold of the black velvet universe. The soul is not shy about self-indulgence in this way because it knows that only by valuing each and every fold can we come to know and love the whole.

The soul loves rich detail, complexity, and messiness; it adores the unpredictable. The soul is willing to see and experience the truth of all of you. Not just what you deem lovable, beautiful, or acceptable. The soul sees beauty in real faces, real bodies, and authentic emotions. The soul says, "Come to the dance; enjoy the feast; it is good."

Wholeness

May love reside in all these realms.

Imagination is what gathers and holds all of the realms of self together. This is why working with personal mythology is an effective means of recognizing, honoring, and expressing the full essential self.

Your essential self wants to experience safety and to flourish in the physical world. Your soul desires to experience the joie de vivre of this extraordinary earthly experience, and your spirit wants to remember the Divine and continue to evolve through the alchemy of life. This is the reason becoming whole is included in the ultimate questions. For millennia, humans have recognized the need to create harmony within the aspects of self.

It is tempting to conclude that something is wrong with us when we experience great disharmony. Yet each of the aspects of self is constantly communicating with us. Our physical health, mental health, energy level, emotions, relationships, money, environments, addictions, goals, and morale all provide needed feedback.

Your personal mythology is where all this plays out and is ultimately expressed in the world. Your outer expression joins the grand creative work of humanity and the world.

This I know for sure. You cannot alter the beauty, power, or innate worthiness of your essential self. You can judge, loathe, or reject yourself, but your full essential self is held safely beyond the reach of your judgment or the judgment of anyone else.

You cannot alter your essential essence. You can try to reject and leave the parts of yourself you hate in a pile on a cutting room floor, but this is an illusion. Repressing, judging, or hiding your essential essence will only result in pain and suffering on some level.

Your essential self remains—whole, intact, full of potential, and as beautiful as it ever was. In our ignorance, we can do many things. We can disrespect or forget, but we can't destroy what the Divine has made in us. Don't believe me? That is why I'm writing this book. I have not always held this deeply sustaining and healing belief either.

We are the only ones who have the power to elevate the value of life to a sacred level. I love to imagine a world in which we are all raised with this fundamentally elevated precept of life. Each of us knowing we were born worthy of the beauty and power that we inherently possess as human beings connected to divine source.

I believe the archetype of royalty is one of the most powerful metaphors for the next evolution of humanity. For some, the captain at sea, the astronaut in space, or the warrior in the battle arena is a more powerful archetype.

What matters is that you identify the imagery and metaphors that light you up. Find the hero/ine who embodies your core values and is manifesting what you most wish to create in your own life. Look for styles of overcoming obstacles that deeply resonate with you, and harness the power of that imagery to embody your full essential self.

Regardless of how your life appears from the outside, your essential self is in a process of evolution. The words and images that you use to feed your imagination are more powerful than our strictly physical or mental selves can fathom. The images and words we live by determine our energetic state of being. Our state of being is what determines the quality of our days, our level of empowerment, and whether or not we view ourselves as innocent or guilty, worthy or unworthy—whether we embrace our birthright or reject it.

ARCHETYPE OF THE HERO/INE'S JOURNEY

Do we even recognize that we are on a hero/ine's journey anymore?

The hero/ine's journey described for millennia remains a powerful metaphor for living a life of meaning and enduring hard times. The hero/ine is another name for the essential self. The heroic journey is the story or adventure of the essential self's evolution.

Nothing can eliminate the pain and difficulty from the life path every individual takes. The heroic journey is the place of sacred evolution. The hero/ine faces trials, confronts the limitations of their original mythology, and emerges changed.

We are always changing and moving in life. Through the power of our creative imaginations, we can be intentional about where we are going and who we are becoming. Collective and personal mythologies and the imagery they contain provide the maps for our journeys through life. Whether told through archetypes, religion, mythology, alchemy, or the hero/ine's journey, the story is always about the sacred evolution of life.

The path of the hero/ine may correspond with prototypical life stages, but I believe we are capable of embarking upon multiple, distinct odysseys during a lifetime. How far we are willing to drop into a quest depends on our belief in our worthiness and personal level of empowerment.

Different metaphors, myths, and archetypes resonate more deeply for different people. Honor the imagery and narratives that harness the most power and inspiration for you. What stories most effectively align your energy, strengths, and essential nature with your core values? What does the hero/ine in you respond to? What image or narrative illuminates a path forward? The most powerful hero/ine archetypes for you embody an energetic state that you are able to access through story, image, and emotion.

Your imagination is able to filter imagery through your physical self, mind, emotions, and spiritual self to create the energetic state of a Queen or King Arthur, a CEO, a saint, or a warrior. From these new energetic states, you operate on a different level and create a new reality for yourself in the world. As the superficial packaging of the hero/ine in the cultural spotlight changes, so do the names and images of the hero/ine. As the richness of our cultural heritage has deepened over time and the marriage of cultural traditions continues, the pool of powerful myths and metaphors has only become deeper.

What does your internal hero/ine stand at attention to? Do you remember a time as a child when you felt the startling, thrilling alignment of your being in response to a hero/ine in a book or film? Likely there is an intimate world within which your hero/ine lives, a specific place and time. Powerful words and phrases—elements of style—can evoke and inspire the same response to this day. What makes you stand a little taller in your nobility? If you could grow to embody the energy of your hero/ine, what would that look like?

Cinderella Soul

The first time I saw the animated Disney classic *Cinderella*, the heroine in me lit up like the north star. I felt like I had found the path straight to heaven. I tied a bandana around my hair and got straight to work cleaning my house. I knew innately that Cinderella was not just dusting curtains as she sang. Her beautiful voice revealed a connection to another realm—dignity and worthiness that were not reflected in her earthly home. Through kindness, grace, gentle strength, and song, Cinderella found her way back to her true home.

Cinderella embodies my core values of faith, beauty, and joy to perfection. With such a beautiful example of who I wanted to be, I truly thought that I would never be tired, cranky, or messy again! As you can imagine, this was not to be the case. My ego used every opportunity to highlight discrepancies between my own expression and the ideal of Cinderella. This is because my ego believed I was unworthy as I was. I went through adolescence, young adulthood, and early motherhood unable to access the inspiration and beauty of my childhood ideal because I was unknowingly holding myself outside of its light. As dramatic as this may sound, I believe I tried to disown every part of myself that did not fit into the Cinderella ideal. Though I was not aware of this at the time.

The reason I allowed my ego to abuse me in this way is because I *believed* judging and rejecting myself was the most effective means of becoming who I wanted to be. Yet a deep part of me has carried the ideal of Cinderella to this very day. As a grown woman, I learned to cherish and protect my childhood love of Cinderella.

We have to find the right relationship to our ideals. We have to create a loving relationship in order to receive the inspiration, strength, and guidance available in our most cherished ideals. Mercifully, beliefs can change, and the ego can evolve. When the ego embraces the truth that we become more of who we want to be when we are loving to ourselves, the voice within becomes kinder.

I now choose to believe I have a Cinderella soul. I have healed the relationship between myself and what my soul clearly longs for. I have intentionally filled the gap between my real, expressed self and my ideal with love.

The beauty of aligning my own mythology with Cinderella is that I have given my life story a beautiful arc. I am heading where I want to go. There is meaning and purpose to the stress, suffering, doubt, and uncertainty I endure along my path. The real life work before me is my sacred work. I am learning daily that faith, beauty, and joy are the way back to my true home.

For every hero/ine, a personal cause gives meaning to all s/he does; there is a person, place, ideal, or way of life that needs protection and care. The meaning, joy, and beauty of life cannot be placed on hold while we engage in our sacred work. The art of morale is the daily resolve to walk in the energy of your core values wherever you go. This is not easy; it is the hero/ine's way. What role does the hero/ine in you want to fulfill?

What does the word nobility hold for you? Whatever image holds the path, the ethical code to embodying your core values and a destination worth fighting for, is a rich metaphor for you. Is it the captain at sea, the soldier in the trenches, or the astronaut in space? The images and language of this metaphor likely create a palpable shift in your energy—a straightening of your back and a lifting of your head and heart.

Within your hero/ine archetype is the template for your personal empowerment. It contains a model of standing in the truth of your core values and creating the life of your dreams—likely (hopefully) a model of the strength to carry humility and mistakes with grace. With your metaphorical castle wall in place, you can choose what to welcome into your interior realm and how you will respond to external events.

You set the law of the land in stone. The hero/ine acts with intention and clarity to serve a personal cause. S/he decides the code of conduct that ennobles his/her path. Immune to distractions, the hero/ine is self-possessed. This I can promise you: there is a hero/ine in you. Today, stand a little taller in your nobility. Welcome the response of the hero/ine within.

The extraordinary success of superhero films reveals a deep need for inspiration, adventure, and empowerment in modern life. Movies are the modern vehicle for delivering the power of the hero/ine's journey. Whether through fantasy or biographical/historical films, we seek meaning in life; we seek models of empowerment and engagement with life.

Harnessing the power of archetypes can help you recognize the hero/ine in your own odyssey. Ancient tales of trial and transformation offer comfort and encouragement to your own journey. They lend meaning and purpose to the struggle, pain, and suffering we each endure. Mythology can connect us to our hero/ine, uniting and communicating a common theme, purpose, and direction.

TALE OF TWO RULERS

The enduring archetype of royalty is a container for the divine truth that we are each sovereign rulers of a realm that is limitless in beauty and abundance. The ultimate goal is to align our beliefs, state of being, and creative powers with this sacred truth.

In a world of suffering, omnipresent evidence of scarcity, and perception of separation, coming home to the truth of our sovereignty comes down to what resides in our personal seat of power. It is time to meet the two great rulers, love and fear.

> *Love:* the energy that composes all life, matter, and consciousness.

> *Fear:* distrust resulting from the use of imagination to separate oneself from love.

Love cannot be fully comprehended or controlled by human beings. Love can be fiercely protective, defensive, unpredictable, mysterious, and uncontrollable. I do not wish to oversimplify love nor claim that it is always clear or easy to follow. Love is expressed intimately through every human being, and every individual has a unique relationship with love.

Love is a far more powerful and complex force than we are comfortable discussing. The way the word is used in poetry, books, and love songs is only part of the story of love. Love is the force behind all of life. It guides our difficult personal evolutions. Love does not always follow our preferences, nor does it protect us from the experiences of harm or pain. It operates beyond our control and full understanding. There is a reason we are afraid of love, why we try to contain it.

Fear is a natural part of the separation we experience from living in intimate form. We will always have fear as human beings. The challenge is not so much to overcome or fight fear as it is to hold our fear in love.

Within the container of human life, fear communicates the presence of potential physical, mental, and emotional dangers. We are meant to listen to, assess, and respond to our fear with intention. Fear provides valuable feedback and navigational direction. Sometimes the presence of fear can even be a sign that we are growing and expanding. Fear has its place in human life.

The goal is to discern when we are listening to fear and when we are listening to love. From this basic understanding we can consciously respond with wisdom.

Many of us have come to a place where we can see the distinctly separate paradigms of fear and love. Yet between the two paradigms, there seems to be a great chasm we don't yet know how to cross. In many ways, the two paradigms offer mirror images of one another. This is because, ultimately, fear is the absence of awareness of love.

Love and Fear Paradigms

Love and fear can be viewed as two distinct rulers. Each ruler operates within a distinct paradigm based on their unique perspectives on self and life. Coming to know the personality, viewpoints, energetic signature, and strategies of our two rulers is extremely beneficial. When we recognize which ruler is currently in our seat of power, we can reclaim our power by choosing to intentionally reside in the paradigm we deem most beneficial. The ruler that resides in our personal seat of power is simply the ruler we trust more in a given situation.

Fear is born of the veil. I believe this is what is meant by the adage that fear is false evidence appearing real. It cannot see through the illusion that there is a scarcity of love, power, and time.

Fear seeks to control because it sees danger and deception everywhere it looks. Fear does not trust life and therefore is on guard against being taken advantage of or being taken for a fool. Fear does not trust joy and ease because these states require vulnerability and faith. Fear trusts "power over" versus "power with" life.

Fear can seek to stay small and contracted or pretend to be big and powerful with explosive energy. Both of these postures are defensive in nature. Fear is defensive because it does not trust the self in the hands of life and is therefore forever attempting to cover its vulnerability.

Love craves freedom and authentic expression because it trusts life. Love sees beauty and sacredness wherever it looks. Love believes in the power of imagination, magic, and miracles.

Fear is the absence of the awareness of love and, therefore, feels like "never enough, never good enough, and never soon enough." Fear is primarily focused on ghosts of the past and projections of the future because it is actually powerless in the present moment.

Love, however, is eternally in abundance and, therefore, is patient and kind. There is no hurry when all is already good. Therefore, love feels like "enough, good enough, soon enough."

Love feels like patience because it feels safe enough to drop down into the full body of time. *Now is good. There is no hurry.* Love fills in the mysterious unknown with faith and trust. Fear skims the surface of time, never allowing the self to relax or enjoy life. Fear fills in the unknown with distrust and vigilance.

You decide which resides in your personal seat of power. You decide by committing to the practice of listening to and honoring the voice of love or fear.

I remember reaching a point in my personal journey where I was consciously aware that I wanted to live, act, and create from the love paradigm. Through much personal work and the insights

FEAR AND LOVE PARADIGMS

PERSPECTIVE	FEAR	LOVE
On self	Believes something is fundamentally wrong with the self. Attempts to cover up and control by judgment and rejection.	Believes the self is worthy as it is. Trusts in expressing self authentically.
Dominant time orientation	Focuses on past and future. Stays on guard in the present to prepare for something harmful coming or something from the past sneaking up.	Focuses on the present. Makes peace with the past, has faith in the future, and recognizes all power is in the present.
Dominant spatial orientation	Steers away from harm and toward safety.	Steers toward what is beloved, desired.
Direction of momentum	Perpetuates vicious cycle.	Perpetuates virtuous cycle.
Use of vital resources	Wastes resources.	Uses resources efficiently.
Reward sought	Seeks safety.	Seeks joy and wholeness.
Abundance	Sees scarcity.	Sees abundance.
Method of influence	Controls by withholding approval or enoughness.	Encourages with approval and enoughness.
Primary mode of operation	Pushes, forces.	Allows, accepts.
Primary life outlook	Distrusts, is cynical.	Trusts, has faith.
Perception of life	Life is profane. Sees life as a burden.	Life is sacred. Sees life as a blessing.
Natural inclination toward life	Constricts: remains small, tight, and safe.	Expands: feels safe to grow, be seen, and be heard.
Mindset	Remains fixed.	Grows.
Relationship to the whole	Sees separation, creates conflict.	Sees unity, creates harmony.

shared from myriad writers, speakers, and artists, I could see pretty clearly that living within the love paradigm made a lot of sense and looked a lot more fun than the guilt-saturated paradigm I was working. I resolved to only speak with love and patience to myself and my family.

But the desire to live from the love paradigm just became the next source of "not enough." I rarely felt I was loving, gentle, or patient enough. I wasn't generous enough. Fear kept me waiting for worthiness and constantly pushing myself harder. Relaxing into enoughness didn't feel safe yet. This was fear's most brilliant strategy yet. Fear whispered *it* was the way, the path to love.

Only the steady application of love, remaining in patience and kindness, eventually begins to transform one's energetic state of being. As we build trust we go from rarely responding to challenges with intention and love to sometimes to most of the time. Any situation or challenge in your life can serve as practice, from creating loving family routines in the morning to completing a manuscript.

Imagine yourself feeling, speaking, and acting from the energy of love in these situations. Love does not only seek an outcome, it embraces the process. After all, the process is life.

The intention to live within love is beautiful. It is a lifelong practice and devotion. Please don't mock your beautiful, positive intentions when you don't yet know how to fully live them out. Fear hates the word practice because it wants certainty. Trust is the gatekeeper of energy, and we have to create trust in the ways of love to actually begin acting and living true to our best intentions.

The Seat of Power

You possess a personal seat of power, a throne, a captain's chair. The art of choosing and maintaining what resides in your personal seat of power is the subject of paradigm shift. By what values do you choose to live? With what kind of energy do you wish to run your life? To what or whom do you want to serve and dedicate your mortal life?

Your personal mythology determines whether love or fear resides in your personal seat of power. Your true beliefs, not what you wish you believed or what you pretend to believe, create a personal system of logic. This personal logic comes from your understanding of the relationship between your self and the outer world. These calculations are personal and can be based in absolutely flawed logic that does not accurately reflect outer reality or true available resources. The point here is that your beliefs are constructing a reality that you are responding to and acting on from within.

You can come to understand your own internal logic, and you are fully capable of informing, educating, clarifying, and rewriting it with intention. When beliefs, relationships, and logic are authentically rewritten, the self can come to a new decision concerning what resides in one's personal seat of power.

All beliefs can be boiled down to either the essence of love or fear. The cumulative balance of the essence from the beliefs that are brought to bear in a given moment or situation determines your fundamental state of being. Put simply, if you were able to quantify your beliefs into 40 percent love and 60 percent fear, you would approach the circumstances before you predominantly from the perspective of fear. I find it helpful to refer to this dominant paradigm as being in my personal seat of power. *Is love or fear residing in my personal seat of power?*

There is a distinct feeling, flavor, and essence when love is in your personal seat of power versus fear. Learning to recognize which ruler is residing in your seat of power offers tremendous value, encouraging you to flow with your state of being or pause to tend to your state of being.

You will follow the ruler that you trust more. When the rubber meets the road, and the perceived stakes are high enough, you will go with what you truly and authentically believe. Fear or love will win out.

Trust is created or blocked by our beliefs and the feedback of our bodies and intuition. Living is always about awareness, assessment, response, and feedback in the present moment. Problems arise when, through beliefs or unprocessed emotion in the body, you become stuck in a fearful state, regardless of current circumstances.

The decision to play safe or live full-out results from calculations of risk and benefit, assessment of your own value and potential, your belief in the possibility of success, and the meaning you assign to potential perceived failure—your current understanding of the resources available to you.

If your personal mythology is hierarchical, you will compare all of these variables with other individuals you believe you are in competition with. Whenever we believe worthiness is conditional, we turn to hierarchy to earn our place.

Cynicism is a form of self-protection. It can disguise itself as rational thought, realism, and the application of intellect to the "facts" at hand. The only problem is that it is just so damn self-fulfilling. You cannot be both cynical and fully empowered. In the end, everyone must decide for themselves how open they will be to life, the grand beauty and the grand suffering. This decision is among the greatest decisions we make in our lives. We want to be aware that we are continually making this decision.

Imagine we arrived at some grand apocalyptic end. Would you feel pride and comfort at how justified your apathy and cynicism had been? Would your last whispered words be "I was right"? Or maybe you would wish you once again possessed the power that lies before you now. Would you choose to actively, joyfully engage in the sacred work of your life? Would the last words that passed your lips be "I truly lived and loved"?

Once you no longer believe that fear is the most reliable or powerful means available to you, realigning with love becomes easier. You genuinely believe more in love. Trusting love feels logical and intuitive. A wonderful momentum toward love occurs once you pass the tipping point in your belief system. You feel better more often and with less effort. However, as living entities, we must always remain in a state of awareness, mindful of our state of being and which ruler resides in our personal seat of power.

UNRAVELING YOUR PERSONAL MYTHOLOGY

All great stories take place within a specific time and place, the details of which create an intimate world—colors, scents, texture, and detail for the imagination to grab on to and bring into its own creation. A storyteller draws the reader in from a vast universe of possibility into a personal world—a unique mental landscape. An intimate world that is filled with protagonists and antagonists, history, love, and fear. This setting is colored and brought to life through the medium of emotional energy. Our personal energy *is* the medium of personal mythology.

A mythology is essentially a story, so let us begin at the beginning. Personal mythology begins to form before our earliest memories.

journaling prompt

Reflect upon the earliest memories of your childhood. Write your story in the voice of your child self to describe your world as you grew up. How deeply you want to go with this exercise is up to you. Even a paragraph can be adequate to capture the overall energy in which you were raised.

Ask your child self:

- Do you feel safe or unsafe?

- Is your family primarily engaged with survival or thriving?

- Do you feel worthy or unworthy of love?

- Is love conditional?

- Do you feel you have to earn love?

- What significant life events (moves, divorce, financial insecurity, illness, or death) is your family going through?

- How does your family respond or react to the challenges it faces?

- Do you feel that you have personal agency?

- Do you have the power to choose for yourself?

- Are you able to dream of and create a life that you enjoy?

During these formative years, the energy of your personal mythology began to color your perception of self and the world. Your energetic home was established. The energy within which you feel most comfortable and natural is directly connected to your formative years. Without considerable personal work and awareness, your signature energetic state of being has likely persisted to this day. This is true even if your circumstances have significantly changed.

Morale is the condition of cheerful, confident engagement with the sacred work of living. For the purpose of understanding the influence our formative years have on our current morale, we will focus on the following qualities from our earliest mythology.

journaling prompt

As human beings, we live in color, not black and white. Yet can you capture the predominant essence of your experience of your childhood? Choose the word in each pair below that captures your predominant feelings about life.

- Safety or danger

- Innocence or guilt

- Abundance or scarcity

- Empowerment or powerlessness

- Acceptance or rejection of self

- Stable or unstable

Beyond the intimate space of your childhood home, consider the influence of community, religion, and culture on your mythology. Reflect on the fundamental components above in relation to the messages you received from your larger community.

Have you ever considered the influence of the decade you grew up in? How did historical events affect your perceptions of life and humanity during your formative years? On the grand scale of humanity, did you see yourself or your family at odds with humanity? Did you view yourself as an important and contributing member of humanity? Was there a sense that humanity was thriving and on an optimistic path to betterment? Or was the narrative saturated in fearful projections for the future?

The answers to all of these questions reflect beliefs, not facts. If you currently believe that you do not have the power to create a fulfilling life, you have not come to hold that belief without reason. Your current beliefs around empowerment reflect your best understanding of your self and the resources you have available to you. When you look with intention, however, you can begin to see evidence of the opposing belief that you are powerful. When you are actively seeking empowerment, you will find there are thoughts, feelings, and actions you can choose to cultivate and practice that make a profound difference in your life. Through steadfast attention to what is within your power, you can gain access to more of your essential resources. You are capable of choosing to believe in and cultivate empowerment.

Mrs. Claus and the Reindeer

When I was in fifth grade, I was chosen to play Mrs. Claus in the school Christmas play. I remember like it was yesterday: sitting cross-legged on the carpeted library floor when the casting roles were announced. As the play did not feature Santa himself, I was cast in the lead role! Completely dumbfounded, I couldn't understand it at the time. How could I have been chosen?

Although I couldn't have articulated it at the time, I had felt invisible at school. I don't think I had ever felt as chosen as I did hearing my name called out for the lead role. For a brief time, the horizons of what was possible for me expanded beyond what I had ever known. I was going to be on stage, and I was lit up. Granted, the stage was an elementary school gymnasium/cafeteria pretending to be an auditorium for the night. But still. Looking back, the only anxiety I can recall about the performance was around remembering my lines.

On the night of the performance, the sea of folding chairs were in place on the glossy gym floor—with the basketball lines peeping out. The side of the room where we normally lined up for lunch was the focal point of the room, the stage. With extraordinarily small fanfare, the show went on. I remembered my lines and returned home feeling quite happy. I slept like a baby without a care in my big, new, beautiful world.

But the next day, I walked into chorus class and immediately noticed the rolling AV stand with clunky TV and VCR. For some reason I cannot now fathom, we were going to watch a video of the performance from the night before. I noticed a boy in my class glaring at me, but I didn't know what to make of it. About halfway through the performance, though, the reason for the boy's anger toward me became clear.

Many of the cast members had been sitting in folding chairs off to the side of the "stage." At one point, I saw the boy, dressed as a reindeer, struggling to escape the tangle of legs and chairs to reach the stage. Meanwhile, I, dressed in my Mrs. Claus costume, was on stage, in a somewhat awkward pause. Then, I continued on with my lines. In the video, the reindeer boy can be seen behind me, angry, mouth hanging open.

As God is my witness, I didn't mean to skip his line, but skip his line I did. As the boy fumbled awkwardly back to his seat, I carried on enthusiastically with my performance. I was completely unaware of anything having happened.

Now back in the chorus classroom, the boy was humiliated yet again, and I was newly horrified. I formed, in those moments that followed, several diamond-hard beliefs. Beliefs that were left unquestioned for decades. Being chosen had been a mistake. I did not belong on a stage. I was a disappointment.

I had hurt someone, and I was deeply ashamed. The feelings of shame and disappointment fused seamlessly with the image of the stage. Tears roll down my cheeks as I allow this painful memory to surface.

Many doors of opportunity slammed shut that day that have remained closed for decades. I wonder now if the precious reindeer boy's path was altered by my innocent mistake. Does he carry a fear of being passed over? Is he unwilling to walk on a stage?

Shame is a painful, ugly thing, so I wrapped mine up in the belief that I suffered from crippling performance anxiety. I'm sure a protective part of myself was confident this belief would keep me far from the shame and humiliation of being on a stage. It worked brilliantly. Despite my love of singing, I haven't even considered performing in front of others. Waves of nausea accompany the very thought of it. I haven't even allowed myself the possibility of being chosen again.

The interesting thing is that now, as I return to that night, I don't remember feeling anxious about being on stage at all. In fact, it was exhilarating. I didn't actually suffer until the following day. Why have I spent all of these years believing I suffer from crippling performance anxiety? Personal mythology isn't necessarily about truth—it is about making sense of the world and our place in it.

Stories, images, and lessons like this one can swirl around beneath our awareness for a lifetime, altering the way we see ourselves and our potential in the world. And sadly, throwing into question what should be an unassailable truth: we are worthy.

Now when I think of that little girl, pouring out her heart on a little stage in a tiny Midwestern town, I am so proud. I wonder if maybe I have been wrong all these years. Maybe there is joy for me in performing. I know I'll never know until I try. A kinder, more encouraging mythology is unfolding. My horizons open just a little more. This is a sweeter place.

FACTS AND BELIEFS

Beliefs are elements of our mythology that we have practiced over and over. They create the major themes, conflicts, and plot at the core of our mythologies. Beliefs also define the major characters of our life and our relationship to them. Beliefs are the medium of creative power.

Facts are occurrences or states that are free from subjective interpretation. Facts can be objectively proven and documented.

In our earthly lives, we are all creating within the context of physical reality. All creation requires constraints. To be *something* means to not be *everything*. Constraints can be seen as the conditions that form a container for and express creative intention. We must include the facts of our circumstances in the creative use of our imaginations. Acknowledging facts also allows us to connect and build with others effectively, and each of us is an integral part of humanity. Nonetheless, the way we position ourselves to facts determines if we are empowered or powerless.

Within your structure of beliefs lie functional relationships. The way your beliefs interface with one another creates either strength, flexibility, and expansion or brittleness, rigidity, and contraction.

Anatomy and physiology provide a beautiful metaphor for how this works. The human body follows an exquisitely complicated and beautiful design. Our bodies were designed to elegantly meet all of our needs on this planet. We have eleven distinct systems to meet all of our physical needs from respiration, circulation, digestion, support, and movement of the body. All of these systems work together and are dependent upon one another for healthy functioning. Anatomy and physiology alone are a complete and holy metaphorical text on divine intelligence.

You were designed for life, and your belief systems aim to meet all of your needs. What are the core beliefs that form your spine, your skeletal system? What are the beliefs that move you forward? What beliefs energize you? What beliefs serve you in eliminating inevitable waste of life such as guilt, disappointment, regret, and anger? Are you aware of where you are better served by flexible or fixed beliefs? The sum total of our beliefs work together, forming a system from which we filter, process, experience, and, through imagination, create our lives. Your true beliefs create your signature way of moving through life. They are deeply personal. No two people possess the exact same set of beliefs.

Our beliefs are always communicating with us. Yet we can experience extreme shock at a deep belief that has been buried beneath our awareness. Yet even the light of our own awareness is enough to begin to disempower limiting beliefs. Operating beneath our awareness is what gives them power.

Our beliefs are not random. Each belief is formed by repeated thoughts in response to life experiences and personal interactions.

As a collective whole, our beliefs indicate where we place the most trust. All beliefs reveal a fundamental trust in either love or fear.

Beliefs form the filters by which we respond or react to all internal and external events. Beliefs answer the question *"What does this circumstance mean for me?"*. They attempt to assess the meaning of perceived reality in relation to self and to position us in the best way possible to present circumstances.

To the individual, beliefs seem to be statements of fact. Beliefs form a wall between what we view as ourselves and all that is not us. This wall is formed at the outer limit of our understanding and perceived power.

Our beliefs are meant to serve us by protecting and guiding us toward the most optimal conditions for the self. By definition, if we believe something, we think and feel it captures the truth for us. When our understanding of truth changes, through education or experience, so do our beliefs. With intention and understanding, harmful and limiting narratives can be released. Life-affirming beliefs can become the bedrock of our personal mythologies.

Remember, at the heart of personal mythology lies an essential relationship between your self and that which you consider to be outside your self. These two constructs and what lies between them are generating your morale. Morale influences how you feel and therefore how you engage with life. How you engage with life determines what you create and the feedback you receive about yourself.

All beliefs contain the energy of creative imagination. Beliefs form a matrix within which we interpret and assign meaning to facts. Beliefs also help us interpret and assign meaning to what we don't currently know or understand. When we recognize our beliefs contain far more than facts, we are left with two essential questions:

- If my beliefs are already composed of creative imagination, how can I reclaim the power to use creative imagination to empower myself?

- Would I choose to believe what I currently believe? In other words, would I choose to hold the facts of my life within my current mythology?

Recognizing which beliefs foster empowerment is essential for cultivating morale. Of the available beliefs pertaining to the situation before us, which beliefs offer hope, possibility, and encouragement? Which beliefs recognize the sacred nature of life? Which beliefs embody the values we choose to live by?

Practicing beliefs that do not provide a positive way forward is disempowering. When we are in a state of disempowerment, we do not use the resources that are available to us to do what we can. When we view our beliefs through the lens of morale, we choose to develop beliefs that reinforce our value and ability to engage meaningfully with life. Cultivating morale is the most sustainable, logical, effective, and efficient mindset for creating what we wish to experience.

Fact	Beliefs
I was born sixty-seven years ago.	I am old. It is too late for me to start anything new. I have more wisdom and self-knowledge than ever before.
There is war.	Humans are violent by nature. We are doomed to repeat history. We are still learning how to resolve conflicts peacefully. Grand, vicious cycles are at play that we can begin to shift with virtuous cycles.
I cheated on my girlfriend.	I am a cheater. I am a horrible person. I have made a mistake that I can learn from. I am not defined by my mistakes. Based on how I am feeling, I know that honesty and fidelity are important values to me.
I have $10,000 of debt.	I am poor. I cannot control my spending. I should be ashamed. I am a powerful person who can make a plan to pay my debts. I am wealthy in love and possibility.
There is evidence of global warming.	It's hopeless. I am too small to make a meaningful impact. Many inspired and innovative individuals are coming together to solve climate change. I am committed to doing my part to care for the planet.

We are fully capable of liberating ourselves from limiting beliefs. We are free to use the tremendous power of our creative imaginations on purpose. As a creative living being, you were born with the ability and right to choose for yourself what you would like to believe about everything. When we are in a state of innocence, we choose to believe what is for our highest good because we feel worthy of goodness.

Beliefs layer, combine, and mix to form relationships. Our beliefs create relationships with self, ultimate reality or God, others, time, abundance, and so forth. Looking at how these relationships are working in your life is an efficient method for redesigning your beliefs. In your current mythology, are your relationships with God, your self, time, or others safe? Are these relationships nurturing or draining? Are you experiencing a sense of empowerment or powerlessness in these core relationships? When we get down to the true core of our belief systems, we find either love or fear.

We have the creative power to align our beliefs with love, to choose the nature of these core relationships with intention. Remember, the facts of our lives are held and filtered by our belief systems and the meaning we assign to the facts. Two souls possessing identical sets of facts would not experience the same reality. Imagine your personal set of facts held in love, a sense of gratitude and abundance versus fear and scarcity. What "facts" are just a memory, a story that could be retold in a new way? What "facts" can simply be released as no longer true or relevant? What is truly present for you here and now? How can you use your current circumstances to grow toward love and embody your core values in this world?

Signature Energy

Your mythology holds the energy of you. The signature energy of your own mythology saturates your state of being, perceptions, and interpretations of reality. It is important to note how one's signature energy remains relatively consistent even through significant external changes. For example, if your signature energy contains anxiety, you usually will find external reasons to explain the presence of your anxiety. You are capable of expanding or shrinking the significance and importance of external sources to match and explain your internal level of anxiety.

Let's imagine that your signature energy is consistently at a seven on an anxiety scale of one to ten. If you have a single external event that can explain your current level of anxiety, you likely won't think much about it. Maybe you perceive two or three smaller sources of anxiety that are adding up to the seven.

When you pay attention to your state of being, though, you can see that you consistently tell yourself a story that matches your energy. This explains how running five minutes late to work can feel like a matter of survival. In this example, your state of being does not feel safe. Even when your environment contains no current trigger for anxiety, the possibility or memory of a trigger will suffice to explain the presence of fear.

You may also stretch or shrink the size and depth of blessings to match your state of being. If your energetic state feels safe and abundant, you can experience this state in most external circumstances.

Your experience of life is more personal fiction than fact. If you have not yet experienced an unsettling shock at the truth of this idea, likely it has not sunk deeply into your consciousness.

Again, two souls possessing the same basic facts of life will create completely different realities for themselves. Thus, understanding our imaginations is vital to personal empowerment. For when we begin to recognize and harness the power of our imaginations in the direction of what we desire to create, the magic begins.

Your Personal Sun

Each of us has a personal sun. Your personal sun resides at the center of your personal mythology, just as the sun resides at the center of our solar system. The light of your personal sun provides essential guidance, clarity, and energy to sustain you. The warmth of your personal sun sustains you in difficult times.

Your personal sun contains everything you authentically care for and hold sacred. It is composed of people, animals, places, values, ideas, imagery, dreams, and causes that authentically bring you joy and meaning.

You mourn when you believe you have lost part of your personal sun. Honoring the pain of losing what provides you with meaning, joy, direction, and love is essential. In times of mourning, provide your self the time, space, and support you need to process your loss. With time you can choose to honor the people, dreams, places, experiences, and ideals you love in your personal mythology. You can continue to carry love for what is no longer present in the physical world, and this love continues to nourish and guide you.

Critically, your personal sun also contains your core values—the eternal ideals that nourish and guide you in every area of your life. Designing your life around your personal sun is essential for cultivating morale.

journaling prompt

Draw a large circle with rays emanating from it like the sun. Fill in this circle with all the people, places, dreams, animals, activities, ideals, and causes that you love and genuinely care about. You can simply write words in the sun or fill it with images. Bringing your focus to what you love is a wonderful way to boost morale. What you place in your personal sun can be as big as "faith" or as small as "the smell of coffee." Some ideas for inspiration are favorite times of day, scents, movies, anything that makes you laugh, music, hobbies, inspiring figures, and authors.

Core Values

Core values are discernable elements of love, like the colors of the light spectrum. We relate to our core values personally, intimately, but they are also universal.

My three core values are faith, beauty, and joy. I have learned that weaving these threads into the fabric of my life is what brings meaning to my life. Faith, beauty, and joy can be woven intentionally into every area of my life from sacred work and relationships to finances and physical health. The presence or absence of my core values in these areas provides valuable feedback.

As a mother, I know I am in alignment with love when I experience faith in my children, see beauty in our relationships, and am present for joy with them. When I experience stress, worry, or frustration in my relationships, it is a sure sign I am in fear. These emotions serve as a call to return to my core values—to love.

I don't believe it is possible to truly experience an absolute ideal in human form, at least not for very long. There is always a space between us and our ideals and dreams. This space is necessary for navigation, movement, creation, and growth. This space is our freedom. We need our ideals as dearly as we need the sun. We need the light, meaning, warmth, purpose, fulfillment, energy, beauty, guidance, and direction that exists *between* us and our personal sun.

Gaining clarity on your own core values provides you with the combination to unlock meaning and love in every area of your life. Below you will find a list of core values. I recommend working through this list and noting the values you resonate most strongly with. From there, keep eliminating values until you gain clarity on your top three—your trinity of core values. While you likely will resonate with many core values, you will find three that hold most of the meaning of life for you. These core values will guide you toward your purpose and sacred work.

Many core values fold within one another. For example, faith holds peace and trust for me, while beauty holds harmony and grace. Joy contains fun and contentment. Your core values are unique and personal to you. The words that hold the most love for you are your core values. Try to release what you think you *should* choose. If you do not find what feel like your core values in this list, many more comprehensive lists are available online.

Core Values List

Abundance	Beauty	Connection
Acceptance	Charity	Courage
Adventure	Commitment	Creativity
Authenticity	Community	Devotion
Dignity	Inclusion	Originality
Faith	Integrity	Peace
Family	Intelligence	Purity
Fun	Joy	Service
Freedom	Justice	Strength

Harmony	Knowledge	Truth
Honesty	Loyalty	Work
Honor	Nature	Wholeness
Hope	Order	

Your essential self always resides fully within the light of your core values. Nothing that has happened to you or that you have done is more powerful or eternal than your core values. This is true because core values and your full essential self are composed of love.

The relationship created between your beliefs about your self and your core values creates your sense of integrity.

Culture and Core Values

Just as individuals carry core values, groups and cultures carry core values. When we are drawn to another culture, we are likely seeking the values the culture embodies. Through sharing in the language, literature, music, style, movies, and food of this culture, we bring more of the essence we desire into our own lives.

Language and expressions are particularly revealing of a culture's core values. In America, we frequently refer to the "good life." In

France, they refer to *"la belle vie,"* or "the beautiful life." In Italy, it is *"la dolce vita,"* or "the sweet life." With beauty as one of my core values, it is not surprising that I am drawn to French culture.

Reading about French philosophy and French people's relationship to time, food, beauty, and pleasure allows me to redesign my own lifestyle with intention. Study of the French language allows me to infuse my core value of beauty into my consciousness. Enjoying French music, art, and fashion in my days allows me to infuse my environment with French style. Through weaving elements of French culture into my days, I experience elevated morale. This is because I am subtly rewriting my personal mythology and weaving my core value of beauty into my life.

Revealing My Own Beliefs

My current beliefs express a stage of my own evolution. The beliefs shared within these pages have helped me cultivate beautiful, consistent, sustaining morale I would not have thought possible even three years ago. We each have the creative power to shift our beliefs to support our own morale.

- The following provides a summary of my own foundational beliefs. Simply by reading a belief I hold, you may become aware of your own beliefs. You will either agree or disagree with my beliefs. This is beautiful, as my hope in writing this book is to help you illuminate your own beliefs and mythology.

- God and life are about the dance and play of energy. When the musician plays with notes and rhythms, the mathematician with numbers, or the painter with colors, they are playing with energy. We are all playing with energy.

- When I refer to life, I am simultaneously referring to God. I believe in the oneness of all; therefore, we are part of God. The terms love, God, life, light, and the Divine are all essentially interchangeable. They are all sacred. I believe in using the words and images that carry the most energy and power in the direction of what you desire.

- We can experience burnout on words and imagery when they no longer influence and inspire us on the same level. The worlds of art, music, religion, science, poetry, and philosophy all serve to keep us in a state of awe and wonder at the miracle of life.

- There is something unique to living entities. Within every cell, there is a "spark," a quality of something that is alive that animates its physical form, for a period of time, in a given space. I choose to believe this spark is divine in nature. It is God. This part of us exists outside the veil of time and space.

- It is not an accident that we exist in a dual state. Part of us is a physical body and bound by the veil of time and space. Part of us is divine, unbound by the veil of time and space. The awareness of this duality prompts many of the existential questions of humanity. I embrace this dual state of human and Divine fully. I do not believe my humanness is meant to be transcended during my mortal life, but embraced. I have faith and belief that the human experience has dignity and purpose.

I believe the solutions to all of the problems facing us individually and collectively reside in love. I believe we are powerful and resourceful enough to indeed address and solve the problems facing humanity. These resources include the clarity and energy that can only be found in love.

All of these beliefs form the framework of my own mythology. I now choose to write sacredness into all of life. This one decision elevates the whole of humanity and life into the realm of worthiness. Seeing all of life as worthy of love has an incalculable effect on morale. This is the reason working with ultimate questions is the most efficient and effective means of working with morale.

THE WORLD YOUR MYTHOLOGY LIVES IN

For many people, the facts of their current circumstances are dire. Some people today are fundamentally unsafe or are deprived of meaningful personal agency. They do not have access to the essentials of physical care. Millions of human beings are living through tragic circumstances.

Harsh realities and the desperate needs of another may be obvious to the outside observer or completely hidden from view. Daily we pass people suffering from unseen abuse, poverty, isolation, or devastating loss. We never know if the person next to us in the grocery line has just lost a child or been told they have cancer. On a greater scale, we are aware of the suffering of great numbers of people outside our personal spheres through the news.

Human life exists within the container of physical reality. Unmet physical and fundamental needs cannot be imagined away. Instead, we must use the creative power of our collective imaginations to raise the value of life to the sacred. From this place, we think, speak, and act differently. We are fully capable of creating peaceful and supportive societies.

Just as the body depends upon the health and well-being of each of its cells, the body of humanity depends upon the health and well-being of every human being. Each of us is called upon to do what we can to lift our fellow humans from the depths of despair.

The truth is our personal mythologies will not provide a fulfilling home if they cannot hold all that we are aware of in a meaningful way. A lack of cohesive logic in our mythology will be felt as dis-ease, or anxiety.

The fear-based belief systems prominent in the world today do not recognize the sacredness of every human life. Current fear-based belief systems based in scarcity justify depriving some individuals of their basic needs. As we cultivate the personal conditions for morale, we simultaneously raise the sacredness of individuals and the whole of humanity.

My aim is not to close a conversation, but to open one. The worldview we live inside and the resulting assumptions we operate from are composed more of imagination than fact. Imagination is not synonymous with deceit or dishonesty. Imagination is divinely given creative power. With clarity and intention, we can learn to harness this power for humanity.

RELIGION

Religions have developed over centuries to answer the ultimate questions for us. They provide a functional understanding of the arena in which we operate—what matters, what to have faith in, and what the scopes of our lives are. For so many people, this framework for living has simply been lifted out. The ravenous void left behind has become a chaotic marketplace for bartering and trade.

Religion cannot simply be removed from our lives without effect. The spiritual aspect of the self needs to be honored to be accessed. We must have language, imagery, and a container large enough to hold the whole of our being if we are to access all the resources we truly possess. The resources of spirit are always there, but we have to write them into our consciousness, our personal mythologies.

If my soul, my life, does not have inherent God-given meaning, how do I earn it? How can I separate myself from the suffering I see and experience? How can I prepare for what is coming? Protect my loved ones? If the meaning of life is my pleasure and happiness, what does my life mean when I am not happy and can find little to no pleasure in living?

For many of us, living without adequate answers to these questions has been painful. The response has been avoiding these feelings through distraction and/or trying to medicate the fear and anxiety of not truly feeling at home in a superficial, secular world.

The idea that we are naive or "woo-woo" because we acknowledge and speak of matters beyond the veil created by our five predominant senses is fascinating. Discussion of the eternal aspects of self is as old as human history.

In modern times, however, we have come to place our trust solidly in the scientific method. With this focus comes many disparaging arguments against consideration of the realms of spirit and soul—the dimensions of self that cannot be directly seen or measured. All of these arguments tend to make one feel ridiculous and afraid of being taken for the fool.

Two arguments against God that were most convincing in my young adulthood are:

- People invent religion because they cannot handle the idea of living in a void. We believe in religion to fulfill a need. We are somehow silly humans trying to comfort ourselves with beautiful lies and falsehoods.

- When we speak of God, we are anthropomorphizing. Obviously, when we see the greatness of the universe and our tiny place within, we are delusional to imagine that God is concerned with us or is able to be understood by us.

Let us boldly name the unspoken fear that lies beneath our apathy and dismissal of the Divine in much of modern life. We are afraid to rely on something that we cannot touch and cannot fully understand. We are afraid to be the fool. We are afraid to place our trust in something that is not real, that we cannot control.

Yet all the inspired sacred texts from every corner of humanity, painstakingly recorded and preserved through thousands of years, surely possess some kind of value for mankind. Sacred texts record the relationship of individuals to the Divine. Sacred texts preserved from around the globe contain universal concepts. I am not speaking from a particular faith, and I am not suggesting that anyone should force themselves into trying to believe something they don't. Authenticity is essential because what we are really working with is trust. I believe the possibility of exploring our relationships to ultimate reality is wide open and ripe with possibility.

Without question, religion has been used to control people to their own detriment. The name of religion has been used to take wealth from the poor and to justify defenseless acts of violence and abuse. These harmful acts were done in the name of religion, but not from the true heart of religious teachings.

Each of the major religions speaks of a whole universe of being beyond the body and concern for its safety. The deepest, most sustaining morale depends upon an understanding of our true power and our sacred connection to all of life. Much of the world has lost the sense that life itself and human beings are sacred.

Wherever there is hunger, homelessness, and violence, the loss of sacredness is revealed. So many of us are beating ourselves up trying to become lovable, valuable, and redeemable. The desire to control what has been viewed as our baser natures has left us in shame and guilt. Our immense personal power is bound up and diffused in the name of humility. Yet we don't have to create worthiness; we just need to remember we are worthy and act from our worthiness. The ego on its own cannot create a sense of worthiness, even though it tries to.

Technological and social advancements of the last few decades have not fundamentally altered the nature of the full essential self. The spiritual energy humans have worked with since before history began is still within you and me. There are many paths for coming to know the spiritual aspect of self and working with its energy. We often need to begin by releasing limiting beliefs about the mere existence of the spiritual self to begin to feel its presence.

The words and images that form your personal mythology can provide the space your spirit needs to feel at home. You can develop a relationship to your spiritual self within your mythology and a means for working with its resources.

Mother Mary

I usually pray to my heavenly Mother and Father. I imagine this helps my limited consciousness come closer to grasping the fullness of the Divine—capturing all that my dualistic mind files under masculine, feminine, and the full spectrum between. I can tell you there is a being that answers to the name of Mother Mary. Just as one aspect of myself answers to Mama, the Divine answers to many names. I see Mother Mary as a face of the Divine. Mary is not contained in the name or image that I hold dear. The spirit and essence of Mary are boundless. Yet for me, the word Mary and her image hold love, beauty, and peace like a glass holds water. In having a personal relationship with Mary, I believe in the intimate relationship people of faith have with Muhammad, Jesus, Buddha, or Krishna.

The Divine can also be accessed through art, mathematics, biology, astronomy, nature, and music. The signature of divine intelligence is found in myriad forms the world over. There is no need to argue over who has the greatest understanding or access to God. The very argument itself is based deep in the belief of scarcity.

Religious Experiences

When I was a little girl growing up in Wisconsin, I desperately wanted to have a religious experience. My soul craved the beauty and eternal goodness of God like a flower craves the sun. I loved the feeling of being in our old church, incense burning, light cast in heavenly colors by the stained glass windows. The hymns seemed to emanate from another realm as the great organ filled the space with music.

There was a language that seemed to only be spoken here as well. Ancient words touched by something otherworldly, deeply comforting and inspiring. The idea that there is great beauty and dignity in humanity provided refuge from the cynicism of the secular world. I had faith that I could cultivate a life of goodness, love, and joy.

Wrapped in the living mythology of religion, I experienced something I am still reaching for today—the holiness of life and a sense of union with the Divine. Yes, the scents and images, the light, the feel of solid wood in the pews, were filling my senses. Sensory input cast upon the veil, arguably hiding as much as it revealed. But this beautiful space was created with holy intention. Sacred time was set aside for deep reflection and worship. The church formed an energetic container, a time and place for intimacy with the Divine. There was a dimension of myself that was touched only in this holy place.

> *"Long lay the world in sin and error pining, til he appeared, and the soul felt its worth. The thrill of hope, God's weary world rejoices."*
>
> —FROM "O HOLY NIGHT"

These lyrics hold a hope so pure and vast that every human being is held in its embrace. The overarching promise is that humanity is worthy, that we are, in fact, on the path to redemption and overwhelming joy! We each possess a divine spark and a special part to play in caring for God's weary world. I experience a magnificent lift of my being in merely typing these words. An energy within myself responds with a heart swelling not accounted for by my physical heart. This is the fullness of self that is not experienced in purely secular life. It is the presence of my spirit. How can we access and express these vast reserves of spirit in the modern secular world?

We need awe, inspiration, comfort, direction, and guidance on the grand scale of religion in order to thrive. Individually and collectively, we possess the energy and wisdom to solve the seemingly insurmountable challenges we face. But we need to write this power and vision into our beliefs and collective mythology.

We don't need to try to be small, afraid of our potential power, or to belittle others. What we need is to step into our empowerment to fulfill the promise of humanity. When the holiness, the sacredness of life, is written into humanity, the soul feels its worth. I believe the next evolution of our spiritual selves is emerging. It remains shrouded in mystery and uncertainty as it has not yet been realized. The events unfolding around us and the challenges they present are calling for a fuller expression of empowered humanity.

What a Mortal Mother Knows of God

You are a child of God. You carry a piece of God's heart with you, just as each of my children carries a piece of my heart. Your beauty, innocence, smile, and laughter are immortal. Through every trial endured, every pain you have known, you have not been alone. God swells with pride at your courage and willingness to shine as your authentic self. Your pain and your joy are shared. You are held in unconditional love, always and forever. All that seems otherwise is but waves on the divine ocean of love.

As a limited, deeply flawed, mortal mother, I can only glimpse how God feels about the children of humanity. I know God does not have only one station for us—a catch-it-if-you're-lucky approach. There is an all-points bulletin. There is a universal language, issuing a universal calling to come home to love.

WHERE SCIENCE AND RELIGION MEET

"Live your life as if nothing is a miracle, or everything is a miracle."

—ALBERT EINSTEIN

The ancient wisdom of the mystics and the findings of scientists are now converging. Science can even be seen as a view of the Divine through a particular set of lenses. When we begin to marry what we know through intuition with knowledge from reason, we gain a greater understanding of ultimate reality.

Science is revealing the face of God in new ways. Quantum theory has demonstrated the oneness of all and the energetic fields within which we all exist. Discrete separation is being revealed as an illusion. This discovery has unified the observations made by mystics for millennia with our rational understanding of the universe. The vast sea of miracles within which we all are suspended is being illuminated by science.

It is fascinating that we generally view a miracle as something that is other than what is. We don't view a flying bird as a miracle, but if a human were to fly, we'd consider that a miracle. We also don't regard the exquisite precision of the human body maintaining homeostasis as a miracle, nor the suspension and orbiting of the planets in our solar system. This is because they simply are.

Humanity has developed vast reserves of knowledge acquired through reason, logic, and the scientific method. This type of understanding is centered on the level of physical reality. We trust knowledge that feels predictable and controllable—safe. Through the study of psychology and nursing I have gained tremendous respect for this type of knowledge. The problem arises when great shadows of doubt and suspicion fall upon all ways of knowing that are not measurable, observable, and reproducible. Most of us have been taught to be distrustful of wisdom and information from outside the realm of sensory input and earthly logic.

In the great process of training our rational minds, many of us have learned to discredit our innate connection to the presence of the Divine, and we suffer for its perceived loss. I don't believe your connection to the Divine needs to look like anyone else's. As a mortal mother, I cannot help but believe reaching for the connection is everything. The bond with each child is unique, personal, told in its own story, and sung in its own song. What matters is that there is love, solidity, dependability, and trust in the relationship. The sense of wholeness and safety that connection to the Divine provides is the elixir of life. The relationship between yourself and the Divine can be cultivated whenever you desire it, just as humans have done for millennia.

The Spiritual Life

Spirituality and reason are not at odds with one another. Cultivating morale is about the practical application of the full self to living well.

There is solid support within the spiritual life that cannot be found outside of it. There is practical wisdom in looking at the logic you are living by and the results you are creating. You do this by coming to understand the way your essential energy is being filled and used. Ignoring the presence of electricity in your home would not be considered reasonable, practical, or safe. It is there and it works. It has been designed for your use.

You are composed of mind, body, and spirit. Acknowledged or unacknowledged, a dimension of yourself exists beyond the veil of perception. The language used to describe it and the framework for understanding the spirit shift, but cultural tides cannot alter its presence and power. It is simply common sense to acknowledge all of what is there—to acknowledge the resources that are available to you.

It is also true that the spiritual path is difficult to navigate at times. Because we are constantly evolving spiritually, sometimes it feels that the ground beneath us grows shaky. We are learning new ways to include our full essential selves into this earthly experience, all the while needing the nourishment and guidance a spiritual life provides. If there were a simpler way for me to discuss morale, believe me, I would. I continue to falter in faith and consistency to this day.

Inherent to earthly life is an element of mystery. All that we can see and know conceals as much as it reveals. Yet I deeply know that we are made for life and designed to use our full beings to thrive.

Acknowledging that part of the self lives outside of time and space and the purely physical can be difficult to discuss in modern life. The topic has become taboo in many circles. The subject is frequently introduced by some awkward reference to being "woo-woo." Your dignity, sanity, or intelligence may be called into question if you speak of such matters. I truly wonder how this can be so. Each of us has had the experience of having all of our physical needs completely met and still experiencing longing for something more. Every day we read of people suffering from depression even though they are safe, wealthy, healthy, and surrounded by people who love them.

What is the part of us that is crying out? What is it within us that can explain the wave of energy we experience when we receive ecstatic or devastating news? Consider the call in the middle of the night: "there's been an accident." Your universe is altered in an instant though nothing has changed in your physical being or environment. Vast resources of energy can be depleted or sustained depending on one's relationship to the spiritual Self.

What is it that humans are capable of tapping into when they are able to achieve extraordinary things for love or a cherished cause? If the mind is simply processing stimuli from the environment, how are we able to imagine realities we have never seen or experienced? I am not writing this with the desire to convert or persuade readers to believe in something they have not experienced. I'm writing this because I know, at some point, we will all face situations when we will need to call upon the deeper self to find meaning in our lives. We will need to access wisdom, strength, and peace that is not present in our physical circumstances to simply carry on.

Without a cohesive spiritual or religious framework within our personal mythology, we are left without the language and imagery to support or even discuss the aspects of ourselves that are beyond basic secular life. When our relationships, shopping, dining, and entertainment don't fulfill us, we feel that something is wrong with us. Self-help that does not acknowledge the needs of the soul or spirit can even become dangerous. Feeling we should simply be positive or practice gratitude can leave us in a state of denial about our true needs. If we have a nice home, family, and great job and still feel a calling for more, the calling is worthy of being answered. We are not selfish or broken to acknowledge a deeper unfolding.

When we don't have the full self and all its resources written into our mythology, we will not understand the needs of the self that are communicating with us or rely upon the wisdom and resources the full self possesses.

Adopting a spiritual understanding that is already established is not necessary. Although, I have personally found tremendous value in the vast reserves of spiritual texts and imagery so easily available in the modern world. I believe God does speak directly through established religions. I also know that God is just as loving and available to those who do not have a traditional spiritual or religious home.

A Steady Transfer of Trust

Safety is a precursor to trust, and trust is a precursor to faith.

Maybe the metaphor of the chasm, the great divide, is not the most helpful in the end. The fear it generates may be dramatic folly. Perhaps the paradigm shift is just that, a gentle shift. An ever-growing trust in the laws of love. A dwelling in the kingdom of love, actively choosing to place love on the golden throne.

Sweet relief washed over me with the release of my chasm metaphor. Yet I also see how that old metaphor has served me well. It allowed me the perspective to see how distinctly different the paradigms are. To know each of the rulers so intimately I can recognize their very breaths in the room. This cherished knowing is worth every moment of suffering in the working out. The energy is not lost but part of this new understanding.

A steady transfer of trust is more helpful than trying to navigate the great chasm between the paradigms of love and fear. When morale is low and we are in a state of deep fear, the leap from fear to love is too great. Remembering that "love is patient, love is kind" reveals the way (1 Corinthians 13:4). Love knows how and why you have come to see yourself and life the way you do. Love sees clearly and deeply the truth that you have always done the best you could. What is one thing you can begin to place in the care of love? Following the path from safety to trust to faith, what is the current focus of your energy? Draw a circle of unconditional love around yourself and invite the truest answer you can hold. Love is the way to love. Trust that any movement toward love will initiate a virtuous cycle.

THE THREE GOLDEN STRANDS OF MORALE

We have now explored how the energy of the essential self is held in personal mythology, and the role beliefs play in aligning our energy with love or fear. We will now turn our attention to the beliefs that have the most bearing on morale.

Three essential beliefs generate morale:

1. You are innocent.

2. You are powerful.

3. You have sacred work before you now.

In the next three sections I will discuss how these core beliefs work together to create hearty morale. You can work with these three beliefs to both assess and cultivate your own morale.

The subtitle of this book is The Art of *Revealing* Innocence, Empowerment, and Sacred Work in Your Personal Mythology. This is because these conditions are always present. We only have to choose to remember, honor, and put them into practice. This is the practice of cultivating morale. Should one strand appear to unravel, the others will sustain you until you remember the truth of your being. Begin with the strand closest to your hands, reach for the next, and braid your golden lifeline anew. It is always there.

When you have left your eternal home of innocence, consciously work to process and clear guilt and blame from your mythology. Your natural cheer and joy of living will return. When your confidence falters, turn to the source of your empowerment—your focus and intention. And when you feel you've lost your purpose, engage with the sacred work before you now, today.

The power of cultivating morale is that it gradually transforms your state of being. Applying the core principles of morale to your life has the power to transform your personal well-being, relationships, and engagement with the sacred work of living.

SECTION III
reclaiming innocence

"Your separation from God is the hardest work you will ever do."

—HAFIZ

THE FIRST OF THE THREE GOLDEN STRANDS OF MORALE we will explore is innocence. Why do I begin with innocence? Innocence is the source of true joy, hope, worthiness, and unlimited possibility. Belief in the power of restoring innocence in my own life was the first critical step toward living from the paradigm of love. When my own energy was saturated in guilt, innocence's duality partner, there seemed to be no way forward.

Innocence is not a state of not knowing, not understanding, or having never experienced something. It is not even a state of having never sinned or been harmed. It is an orientation to life that resides in a state of trustful being. Innocence is freedom from judgment, guilt, and blame. First experienced in not knowing, innocence is then re-experienced from knowing more deeply. The renaissance of innocence is one of the greatest joys of coming home to love. However, first there is a journey, an odyssey if you will.

We must explore how we believe we have lost our innocence. We use guilt, shame, judgment, and blame on ourselves and others for a reason. The reasons we trust and turn toward these tools can be found in our own belief systems. In this section, we explore why we willingly give up our sense of innocence and what we believe we gain in doing so.

In a state of innocence, we have access to the fullness of our true potential. The perceived loss of innocence robs us of the unconditional worthiness that is so foundational to hearty morale. We have to believe that life is worth living and that we are worthy of the sweetness of life to truly experience sustainable, lifelong morale.

No belief will offer as much relief, hope, and spaciousness in your being than the belief in innocence. Belief in the idea that beneath all the drama and power struggle at the surface of your awareness, you are worthy of love as you are. That you can trust your natural instinct guiding you toward wholeness and well-being. Following your internal guidance is, in fact, the most efficient and joy-filled way to both *be* and *do* in life.

FEAR AS A METHOD OF CONTROL

An important role of both culture and religion is to manage the uncertainty of large numbers of powerful individuals—each possessing free will—into a cohesive whole. It could be argued that procuring safety for individuals is the primary goal of civilizations. We are willing to give up freedom in order to achieve a sense of law and order. As long as people believe that fear is the most powerful means of establishing order, that is the way they will trust.

The problem with trying to control by use of fear is twofold: first, as humans, we will all sin, and second, defining ourselves by our mistakes is a powerful misuse of creative power. Attempting to do the right thing out of fear of punishment for doing the wrong thing begins a vicious cycle. A power dynamic of resistance and counterresistance begins. We forget entirely that we wish to tell the truth simply because it feels good to be in a state of innocence. Instead, we want to tell the truth to avoid punishment.

The fundamental belief embedded in this cycle is that we cannot trust our essential natures. Therefore, we exert tremendous effort into using control, judgment, and manipulation to simply do what is inherently good. Honesty is already a reward in itself. This is how fear looks in practice. Fear as a means of motivation or control is incredibly inefficient.

There is nothing to gain by imprisoning souls with infinite potential in fear. Whether we are holding ourselves in prisons of guilt and shame or others in blame and judgment, the effect is the same. We are not free. We are held in the painful and disempowering drama of victim and perpetrator.

When you embrace your essential self, your construct of life and all of humanity rises to the level of sacred. From this place, you no longer desire to degrade your soul or your humanity by enslaving it to the ways of guilt and fear. You fundamentally trust and believe in the ways and power of love. It no longer feels like you are fooling yourself into believing or feeling something that is too good to be true. The virtuous cycle of love begins to unfold in your life. The gift of all the years living saturated in fear is that you know—on a cellular level—the taste, flavor, and feeling of that energy.

The Flower

The metaphor of a simple flower in a pot is the most elegant one I know of to illuminate the difference between trusting in love and trusting in fear. We innately recognize that the divine intelligence encoded within the flower seed is to be trusted. If we wish to see this flower grow into maturity and blossom, we need to provide the necessary conditions for that process to unfold naturally.

What does a living plant need to thrive? It requires life-giving energy from the sun, clean water, and fertile soil. Its tender shoots require shelter from the trauma of strong winds. All of these must be provided within the range required by the individual needs of the plant. How much water? How much sun? The answers are in the thriving of the plant. There is no need to argue with the needs of the plant. It is crystal clear that this would be the greatest folly and waste of time. Violence against the plant, rushing the plant to grow, or judgment of the plant are acts against nature.

When you begin to see yourself through the eyes of innocence, you will see how clearly this also is true for you. You will want to construct an environment to foster the natural unfolding of the divine nature that is in you. Your morale is a measure of your own thriving. When your morale is strong, your days contain joy and cheer. You possess confidence in your ability to express your full self in the world, and you are engaged with life in a joyful, meaningful way.

LA GRANDE BEAUTÉ AND LA GRANDE SOUFFRANCE

As expressions of God in intimate form, we experience both the great joy and beauty—*la grande beauté*—and the great suffering—*la grande souffrance*—of life. Neither our belief systems nor our egos can separate us from the truth that we will suffer. Yet our belief systems and creative power can open us up more fully to experience the beauty, joy, and awe of life.

Life exists within infinite layers, inner and outer circles of the Divine. We are living literally suspended in a matrix of miracles. Yet, like a fish in the ocean who cannot sense the water, we can miss the Divine because it is ever present. It simply is reality. What if science is actually a catalog of miracles? If we can capture the emergence of a butterfly from its cocoon in time-lapse photography, does this mean it is not a miracle? If we can dissect the cocoon and the tender flesh within, does this make it science?

There is enough beauty in any moment to ponder for all eternity, ample evidence in a thimble to prove God's ever-present love. We are composed of and suspended in a matrix of the Divine. That's why it's so hard to see when we are looking for evidence. There is always a part of each of us that remembers this truth.

Look for the times the Divine peeps out from the mundane and calls to you—in a song, the eyes of your children, the beauty of evening light, the revelation of a new season, a soulfully cooked meal—and answer. Answer with your presence, awe, and delight.

We have to dwell in our spiritual senses to perceive the beauty and the miracle of life. Once we have opened ourselves to the memory, the golden signature of God shines through absolutely everyone and everything. I can't imagine the look on our sweet Lord's face when we are asked, "How could you have missed my heavenly embrace?"

Without the active choice to focus on *la grande beauté*, *la grande souffrance* will likely become the choice made by default. The loud and ever present voice of the ego wants to keep us safe at all costs. Using our own creative powers to block the beauty and joy of life is entirely possible. In fear we can become focused solely on attempts to avoid suffering, and in fear we attempt to assign blame for our suffering.

The fact that life is hard does not mean that something is wrong with us. The fact that we suffer and cause suffering to others does not mean we are unworthy. Ignorance, complexity, trials, and suffering are all built into the human experience. One critical role of mythology is to help us find meaning in our suffering and remain open to the great beauty of life. What do we choose to make the fact that life is hard and that we will suffer mean?

There are two types of suffering, *la grande souffrance* and drama. *La grande souffrance* is inseparable from the intimacy of life. We cannot ignore that it exists because it is self-evident and omnipresent. If we love and open ourselves to life, we will eventually experience suffering and loss. We know that we and all we love are vulnerable. We are mortal.

Yet it is equally true that if we don't love or open ourselves to life we will suffer. The suffering born of the intimacy of life cannot be written out. It's part of the human experience. Defining our relationship to both *la grande beauté* and *la grande souffrance* can be seen as one of the most fundamental tasks of our personal mythology. What meaning do we find in suffering, and what can we turn to for comfort, strength, healing, and guidance? How do we stay open to the great beauty of life?

Drama, on the other hand, is all the unnecessary suffering we add through mismanagement of our imaginations and minds. Much of the suffering we experience in life is due to drama. We experience a great deal of suffering because of things that have already passed or that will never actually happen. I will devote time to the topic of clearing drama in the empowerment section. For now, just know that drama is the use of imagination to make anything we want to accomplish, feel, experience, or accept more difficult. It is the expenditure of our vital resources of time, focus, energy, and imagination to create what we do not want.

Cultivating morale in your life is not intended as a form of hiding from *la grande souffrance*. It is an intentional strategy for remaining grounded in *la grande beauté*. We cannot pretend to be ignorant of the equation of our vital energy. One cannot endlessly make withdrawals from one's physical, emotional, mental, and spiritual reserves. To remain enthusiastic and engaged, we must be actively drawing from the infinite source of love.

As the noble cell illustrates, life requires give and take—rest and activity, inspiration and expiration. We can only work and give so much of our resources before we begin to experience a decline in healthy functioning. We must balance what we receive and give in life. The good news is that there is truly an abundance of beauty and goodness in life to draw strength from.

> *"Those who contemplate the beauty of the earth find reserves of strength that will endure as long as life lasts. There is something infinitely healing in the repeated refrains of nature—the assurance that dawn comes after night, and spring after winter."*
>
> —RACHEL CARSON, *SILENT SPRING*

Nonetheless, we cannot ignore the truth that alongside the great beauty of life, there is great suffering. Alongside your significant power, there is the great power of the mysterious Coauthor. We also know deep down that if we possess great power, so do all the people with whom we share this planet. We cannot claim our own vast stores of power without acknowledging the vast stores of power all others possess. In acknowledging our individual limitations, we are able to feel the solid ground of truth beneath our feet.

From where humanity is in our current evolution, imagining all of our collective power unleashed upon the world is naturally scary. Surely, there is a gradual process of humanity becoming more empowered. In fact, I believe we are living and evolving through this process now. Each of us individually must decide if we will become empowered in love or, through fear, remain disempowered.

Here's the thing: if you fear what lies within you, you will fear all that surrounds you. If you question your own nature, you question the nature of all that comprises the universe. It is all one. Divine intelligence is the energy behind all that is; it collects and solidifies as the physical reality around us.

How do we reconcile the great beauty of life with the great suffering? How can we consciously direct our focus toward joy and away from fear? How do we gain the courage to engage in sacred work? How do we experience deep and abiding faith in this troubled world, amongst our deeply wounded humanity? Ultimately, how do we transfer trust from fear to love? The answers to these questions lie in the cultivation of morale through virtuous cycles.

VICIOUS AND VIRTUOUS CYCLES

As we have already explored, to be alive is to be in constant motion. We are always evolving or regressing in the temporal and spatial realm. This momentum can be described as having navigational value. Are we moving toward fear or toward a state of greater love? If we keep thinking, feeling, and doing the same things we are now, will we experience more joy and peace or more pain and scarcity? One benefit of the simplicity of dualistic patterns is that they can provide clarity and navigational assistance.

This is the fundamental crux upon which morale rests. Living with fear in your personal seat of power *is* a vicious cycle. Living with love in your personal seat of power *is* a virtuous cycle. Honoring morale is the pragmatic path to living in greater and greater alignment with love.

I believe we are instinctively aware of what is in our seat of power. Therefore, we are aware if we are moving toward greater abundance and well-being or toward scarcity and illness. This underlying knowledge affects both our ability to experience cheer and our self-confidence. This is why understanding what energy is driving us is fundamentally important for morale.

You cannot remain still in life. You are either contracting or expanding. Sadness, anxiety, darkness, guilt, and despair are the result of the awareness that we are contracting. We know we are moving away from what our hearts most desire. Our morale reflects this inner knowing and is a call to the conscious self.

One reason you use judgment and blame is to separate yourself from suffering. Judgment and blame can be used in an attempt to separate you from the oneness of all. Another way we try to use judgment and guilt is for motivation. We think if we feel bad "enough" as we are, we will try harder to measure up to the standards we or others hold for us.

However, judgment is a bit like a drug in that the more you use it to motivate yourself or others, the more you need to achieve the same effect. As with a harmful drug, the toxicity and dependence grow until your natural, loving forms of motivation begin to seem too good to be true. How can you trust joy, acceptance, patience and loving encouragement to get you where you want to go? Living from fear is a vicious cycle, and this cycle feels as if it is drawing you into a tighter and tighter dead end.

The moment we choose to honor our own morale, we begin a virtuous cycle. We are reaching for innocence and empowerment while embracing the sacred work before us now. Even when we are very low and experiencing deep pain, we can be aware that we are moving through pain toward something better. The thinnest thread of morale pulls us in that direction—through grief, a spiritual crisis, the pain of creating a new life, or giving birth to a new self—to the other side.

Vicious and virtuous circles operate on all levels of life, from the cell, the self, our relationships, humanity, and Mother Earth herself. Regardless of the depth, scale, or seriousness of a vicious cycle, the only path out is engaging in a virtuous cycle. The first critical act is to decide to disengage with the vicious cycle and commit to beginning a virtuous cycle. We do this by remembering and honoring the sacredness of life. Believing in the power of virtuous cycles is believing in the power of innocence.

In whatever situation we face individually or collectively, some variables are within our control and some are not. Some outcomes we desire, and some we do not wish to come to pass.

We must first take the time to understand and gain clarity on the challenge or situation before us. What is the source of fear generating the vicious cycle? Is it belief in scarcity or the power of judgment to keep us separate and safe? Wisdom comes from truly aiming to understand the narratives at play, assessing all available information and resources, and gaining clarity on what we wish to create.

Using all available information, resources, and the creative power of choice, we are empowered to move toward our desired outcome. We must choose to initiate and engage in virtuous cycles. Step by step, day by day, this is how the seemingly impossible is achieved and the process by which all that cannot yet be seen is created.

Freeing ourselves from judgment and fear, residing in innocence, allows us to see most clearly where we are and where we want to go.

In human life, there is no absolute state of love or fear. Both forms of motivation have their place. When we are not acting in alignment with love, it does not feel good. The feeling of guilt can be a valuable call to assess our actions and motivate us to make amends. Problems arise, however, when we stay in feelings of guilt or blame beyond the point of bringing awareness to and committing to a course of action to realign with love. We are not intended to reside in states of guilt or blame. When guilt becomes our state of being we are likely suffering from issues of worthiness. When blame and anger become our state of being we are likely dealing with issues of empowerment.

What is your primary motivation in life? Are you consistently placing love or fear in your personal seat of power? On a daily basis, are you experiencing the feeling that you are joyfully moving toward something desirable in freedom or being driven from something painful in fear? Are you relying more on guilt, judgment, and blame or innocence and compassionate understanding to guide you through life? With the smallest amount of attention, you can begin to recognize the signature energies of love and fear. The knowledge of which energetic state you are in is the first step.

The Baker and the Cake

The metaphor of the baker and a cake beautifully illustrates the possibility of choosing innocence. If you were to view your life as a cake, you might be very disappointed to realize that you had mistakenly added vinegar to your cake batter. You might try to deny or cover the flavor of vinegar, yet it would remain. If you believed you had only one chance to bake a delicious cake, you might despair over this error. You might not believe in your ability to ever make a cake you can enjoy or be proud to share. But the cake does not define the baker; it is simply an expression of the baker in a given time and place. The baker is the creator of the cake and is always free to begin again, to gather from the pantry the finest ingredients available, and, with very few, simple ingredients, create a deeply satisfying cake.

In life, the adding of the vinegar may seem more complex. Perhaps it is viewed as a sin or an indication of a character flaw. Maybe you have suffered through trauma or violation of your sacred rights. This is where we have to look deeply into the design and purpose of the mythology we currently hold as truth. Many prominent beliefs in cultural narratives make you believe that you, the baker, have been permanently altered, defined by a sin or painful experience. That you the baker have been defined by a bad cake. I believe this prominent narrative is told in an attempt to prevent people from making mistakes, the rationale being that fear of being labeled will keep us on the straight and narrow. Yet the cost to human potential from this method of control is incalculable.

You always possess the power to grant the baker the gift of a fresh start. Begin your story anew in the voice of your heroic self.

THE HEROIC JOURNEY HOME

To reclaim innocence requires that you transfer your trust from fear to love. The essential self does not need to be imprisoned in a cage of guilt, shame, judgment, or blame. Tremendous joy and power are released when the essential self is freed to live in innocence.

There is no question of the courage, persistence, and stamina required to shift where you place your fundamental trust. This is heroic work. When you begin to shift your trust to innocence you are cultivating an interior reality that is not yet reinforced by your environment. You are learning to embody ideals that are in opposition to what your environment is presenting to you as reality. The hero/ine is able to find the inner fortitude to live from a realm of innocence, abundance, and empowerment, thus creating a new physical reality.

There is no need to worry, though, for when we are looking, we find we are surrounded by heroes and heroines. They have left detailed accounts of the journey for millennia. Your journey won't look exactly like anything you've ever seen before, because it is uniquely yours. The important thing is to remember, recognize, and honor the heroic path *you* are living. When our own lives are hard, it is easy to feel that something is wrong with us. The truth is sometimes being human is brutally hard. It doesn't mean that we are broken. We are on the journey of a lifetime.

In the past, I viewed physical reality, based in scarcity, and the spiritual realm, based in abundance, as separate realities. The physical taking precedence whenever I perceived that safety was on the line. At times of stress, we are able to see what truly resides in our personal seat of power. Will we seek to separate ourselves through judgment? Or see our oneness through seeking to understand?

How do we reconcile the abundance mindset of love with the need for personal scope? The limitations of human time, energy, and focus in the physical world are constraints to be respected. These constraints can be seen as forming a container. In times of great stress, this container can feel like a crucible.

What do we do with the impulse to protect our own children, plan for our own hard times? As physical beings we see the physical first. God meets us where we are. The natural condition of humans is to be concerned for the physical self and the need for safety and security. What is the point of the duality and the struggle? How do we reconcile the physical and the Divine? These are the questions that burn beneath the secular surface of life. How do we honor the full essential self in human life?

For me, the answer lies in love. We love the Divine *through* loving our intimate, personal lives. We honor our dualistic state by remaining in love—the intelligent, divine energy that composes all. Morale is the state of being oriented toward love and engaging with the sacred work of living from where we are, now.

The Abraham Hicks Emotional Guidance Scale is an invaluable tool for monitoring personal morale. It offers hope by providing navigational guidance. No matter where we are on the scale, we can experience a boost in morale when we orient ourselves toward love.

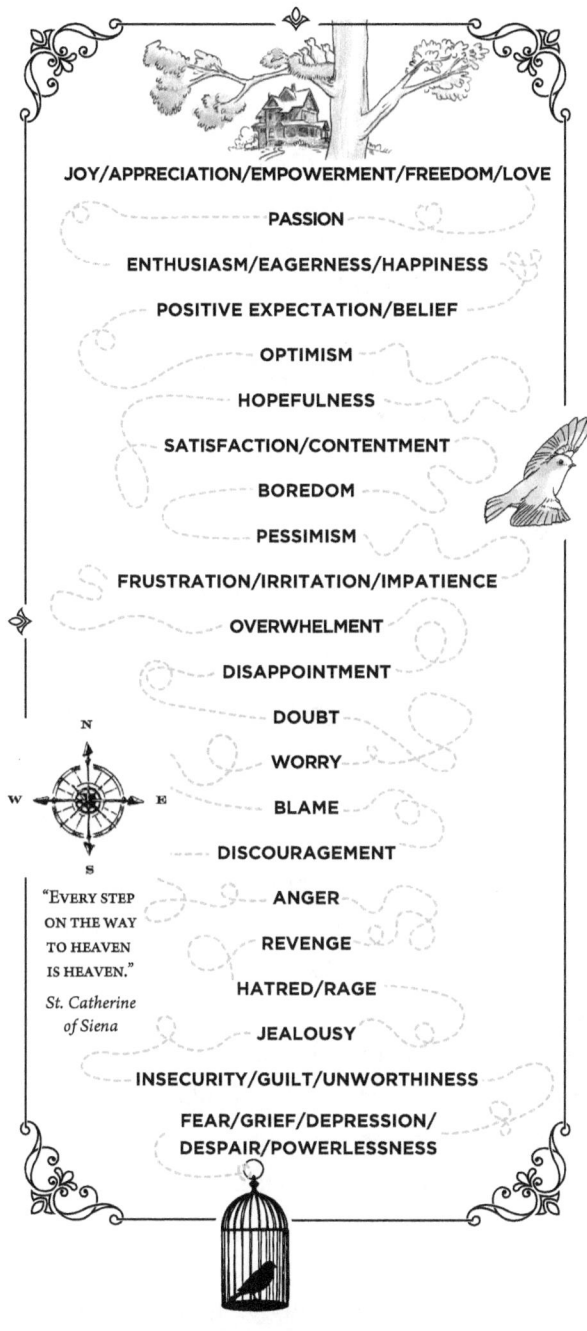

JOY/APPRECIATION/EMPOWERMENT/FREEDOM/LOVE
PASSION
ENTHUSIASM/EAGERNESS/HAPPINESS
POSITIVE EXPECTATION/BELIEF
OPTIMISM
HOPEFULNESS
SATISFACTION/CONTENTMENT
BOREDOM
PESSIMISM
FRUSTRATION/IRRITATION/IMPATIENCE
OVERWHELMENT
DISAPPOINTMENT
DOUBT
WORRY
BLAME
DISCOURAGEMENT
ANGER
REVENGE
HATRED/RAGE
JEALOUSY
INSECURITY/GUILT/UNWORTHINESS
FEAR/GRIEF/DEPRESSION/DESPAIR/POWERLESSNESS

"EVERY STEP ON THE WAY TO HEAVEN IS HEAVEN."
St. Catherine of Siena

From Ask and It is Given *by Esther and Jerry Hicks*

The Abraham Hicks Emotional Guidance Scale provides an image and model for the emotional journey toward love—our true home. When we honestly determine our current emotion on the scale, without judgment, we can have a sense of where we are and where we want to go. These two points of navigational reference are the fundamental requirements for empowerment. Where we are empowered, there is hope, motivation, and confidence. Cultivating morale is possible even when we are experiencing acute or prolonged, habitual, lower-energetic states of being.

Another gift of the Abraham Hicks Emotional Guidance Scale is that it helps visualize the steady transfer of trust required to make the paradigm shift from fear to love. There is not a great chasm after all; there is a known path. A path complete with individual stepping stones, where each step up the scale corresponds with increasing levels of morale.

While we can observe many shifts throughout a typical day, the important question is "Where am I currently living most of the time?" Reflect on all the key areas of your life and look for patterns. For example, let's say you identify impatience in your health, work, and relationships. This is something you can begin to work with. Look to your personal mythology, beliefs, and thoughts. What is the source of this impatience? Likely you will find a belief in scarcity behind it. You believe you are not making enough progress, soon enough, or the progress is not good enough.

Well-being and abundance flow most efficiently and reliably from love. Where are you holding your self, finances, health, or relationships outside of love? Let's say for example you have the belief that to be worthy, you need to be in a romantic relationship. If you are not currently in a romantic relationship you may find you don't approve of yourself as you are. Another way to understand not approving of yourself is to see that you, through your beliefs and imagination, are holding yourself outside of love.

The irony is that the worthiness, acceptance, and joy you are seeking can only be found in love. Many people experience worthiness, acceptance, and joy who are not in romantic relationships. This is because their beliefs, their personal mythologies, are in alignment with love in this area.

Using the same example you may experience jealousy when you see a couple in love. The presence of jealousy is very natural given your belief that someone else has something you need to feel worthy or happy.

We never need to judge our emotions; we only need to learn to listen to them. They are there to guide us toward love. The feeling of jealousy is unpleasant, however, and difficult to accept. Individually and collectively we reject and judge jealousy and may therefore try to reject the part of ourselves that experiences jealousy. Rejection means we are not accepting and therefore not listening to critical guidance. It is very difficult and inefficient to try to get where we want to go when we don't accept or honor where we are.

We do not need to react to all of our emotions. When we fear we cannot handle our emotions we resist them, keeping negative energy trapped. Granting ourselves time and space to feel and process our emotions allows us to return to our natural state of innocence. It is safe and vitally important to listen to all authentic communication from the full essential self. Once we have received information, we are then empowered to assess our options and respond with intention.

SINS, SIRENS, AND STORY

We both design and navigate the odyssey of our lives within our personal mythology. Through the filter of beliefs, we set up the challenges we face becoming who we are evolving into. Through the story of our hero/ine self, we define our own level of worthiness, state of empowerment, and value to the world outside of ourselves. An essential part of moving forward in our personal odysseys is understanding where we are coming from. We must identify the stories we tell that keep us feeling unworthy of innocence.

Sins

Oxford Language's first entry of sin is as follows.

Sin: an immoral act considered to be a transgression against divine law.

If a sin is a transgression against divine law, this means to act against love. Through a process of dignified confession, I have been able to face my history. Although not comfortable or joyful in remembering, I can safely see the darkness I have experienced and the mistakes I have made. I now understand that fear has been behind all my sins. I recognize that fear is behind the sins and mistakes of others as well. I know this because there is no "getting away with" acting from dishonesty, unkindness, or scarcity.

If you are acting in a fearful way, then you are *in* a fearful state. If someone could feel safe to tell the truth, be kind, or dwell within the beautiful state of generosity, how could they choose otherwise? When we sin, it is because we do not feel worthy or capable of dwelling in love. Joy, abundance, peace, and innocence are rewards in and of themselves. No amount of blaming or abuse will bring the self to worthiness.

On some level, I have committed all of the following sins:

- Dishonesty in the face of fear

- Weakness in the face of fear

- Belief in scarcity

- Self-preservation at the expense of another

- Hiding in the face of fear

- Avoidance of personal responsibility

- Violence

- Self-medicating the pain of living

- Stealing

- Cheating

- Despair

- Hypocrisy

There is no need to compare your sins with mine or anyone else. The need to compare is born of fear. Fear seeks a reason to keep you or others outside the circle of unconditional love because it cannot trust unconditional love. Fear is the absence of faith.

We are all human by divine design. We all sin. The question is what do we choose to make this mean? For me, it means we are evolving. We are an essential and intimate part of divine alchemy.

How can we come to truly believe that we have always done the best we were able to at the time? One of the first variables to consider is the primary state of being you were operating within when you sinned. By this I mean were you operating from a survival state or a thriving state? This is not as simple as identifying whether your life was literally at stake when you were making decisions. Were you operating under a physical or psychological state of survival? Chronic mental, physical, and psychological stress create the physical, mental, and psychological state of survival. Beliefs alone are powerful enough to create a chronic state of fear, stress, and vigilance.

Imagine that you genuinely hold the following sentences to be fact: If you steal you are a bad person. If you have ever stolen, you are a thief and a bad person. If you have ever lied, you are a liar and a bad person. If you are a bad person, you do not deserve love, acceptance, or happiness.

It is very easy to see how you would feel tremendous fear about admitting the truth of having stolen or lied. By definition, this belief system does not create an internal environment of safety. These beliefs will directly translate into unsafe thoughts and feelings and the physiological state of stress. How many times have you experienced the emotions of stress and fear when, in reality, you were perfectly safe? That which is in the mind of the individual is quite literally as real as what is evident in the physical world.

Of course, we aim to have moral courage in whatever circumstances we find ourselves. We want to trust ourselves to embody our core values no matter what the external environment presents. In hindsight, you may view your failure by saying, *If I had truly done the best I could, I would simply have told the truth.*

Here I ask you, if you could have acted in accordance with your deepest values, don't you imagine you would have? Your internal or external sense of safety, fear, or lack of clarity were an obstacle that you did not know how to overcome at that time. Your ability to see that clearly is essential in growing on your path of empowerment.

Fear would have us believe that if we label and judge harshly enough, we will not make the same mistake again. From the perspective of fear, punishment is seen as the most effective way to control. If it is in your power to punish, does it not follow that it is in your power to control?

The essential question is this: if fear keeps you from initially behaving in accordance with your higher ideals, will the accumulation of more fear genuinely make it more likely that you will act from your higher ideals in the future? It is my experience and understanding that this is not the case.

Believing myself to be lesser, weaker, flawed, and broken has not yet brought out the best of who I am. If you have not yet spent decades devoted to this flawed idea of self-management, please believe me—your results will not change in the direction you desire through commitment to self-condemnation and abuse.

The energetic sludge of resistance and counterresistance, self-deceit, judgment, and blame acts like quicksand, leaving you nothing to hold on to. Every effort results in your sinking deeper and deeper.

Your worthiness, essential nature, or your core values are not the issue; the source of suffering is your belief in fear as an effective means of self-management. It is the questioning of the fundamental value of your self.

Through the self-manipulation and judgment that results from fear, we lose our connection to our fundamental innocence. We no longer have a sense that we are wholesome. Eventually, even our natural instincts are surrounded by a dark distrust. We feel we cannot be trusted, that we are fundamentally wrong.

Fear grows, and justification for distrust and self-abuse grows right along with it. Yet, just as there is a path into despair, there is a path that leads out of despair. We can grow to once again trust what feels good. We can choose to believe in our own innocence and regain faith in our worthiness.

Regardless of the judgment that surrounds you from others, you have the power to create an internal state of safety for yourself. Doing so is a fundamental act of self-love. A radical willingness to see your truth clearly grants space and authority to your higher self to speak to you where you actually are.

What does love believe is the way of aligning our behavior with our highest ideals? I believe the answer is understanding self through safety and honesty. Through the compassionate understanding of what disempowered you in a given time and situation, you are able to grow in clarity and courage.

Where once you were left shackled to guilt and shame, you can erect a metaphorical lighthouse. A lighthouse alerting you to the rocks you once crashed upon, lighting the sirens whose call you answered. You have condemned, punished, and abused yourself based on a belief that doing so would keep you from making the same mistake again. Fear trusts judgment and punishment, whereas love seeks to understand, resolve, and reclaim your precious light and energy to do good.

If you have made the same mistake time and again, you have suffered the same consequences time and again. It is time to release this pattern. Comfort yourself with the knowledge that you have learned these lessons on a cellular level. You can hold compassion for others and shine light for them when the opportunity arises.

Through cultivating courage and the gift of divine grace, I have experienced redemption. By redemption, I mean that my essential resources are now freed to use with intention. I know that God did not place us here to feel like broken failures, unequal to the challenges of life. We are meant to experience innocence by always returning to love. Any shadow that we experience between ourselves and God, we have willingly placed there.

The process of clearing the space between ourselves and God is our spiritual practice. This practice keeps us oriented toward and in a state of innocence. Our energy and focus are free to be realigned with love in the present moment. It is the most effective and efficient method for finding the love and joy we are all truly seeking.

DIGNIFIED CONFESSION AND A NOBLE PATH FORWARD

"Do the best you can until you know better. Then when you know better, do better."

—MAYA ANGELOU

An important role of religions has been the spiritual rite of atonement. As a little girl, I remember going into a tiny, dark, ornate wooden room to make my first confession. Already saturated in guilt and perfectionism by the tender age of eight, I was not about to reveal my deepest, darkest secrets. Quite ironically, I made up fictional sins. I went with what I thought to be both believable and yet not too shocking. I debated nervously in the line of children until the moment I entered.

I remember it like it was yesterday. The solemnity of the darkness, the metal screen, and the unmistakable, ever-present smell of incense. I was startled by the closeness of the priest and how well I could make out his features through the metal screen. When the time came, I blurted out the ridiculous confession that I had taken the Lord's name in vain. I was fond of the expression "holy cow" at the time and had been told it was wrong to say. Looking back, I can see that I hadn't yet cultivated trust with the priest or the process of confession. Honesty without some measure of safety is nearly impossible. It is heroic work at best.

Now I can see beauty in the formal act of confession. We need a way to release the energy and story of self-judgment. Most religions allow for a season of reflection and atonement—looking deeply to understand our mistakes, envision our spiritual path, make amends, and actually clear the energy tied up in guilt and blame. We are then granted a fresh start, a clean slate.

For me, this essential work has become mostly an interior process. I create a field of unconditional love and imagine casting my sins and errors upon it. This initial separation of guilt from the essential self is the first step to seeing with clarity. Held in internal safety, I can begin to look with honesty at whatever situation is troubling me. The essential self is not meant to be defined and limited by our mistakes and sins.

My ego is still very attached to the idea of being "right." I believe being right is the ego's version of innocence. The ego defends and denies because if it hasn't actually done anything wrong, it remains innocent.

My ego is getting better at letting my full self hold the truth of my life. This is a slow process of building trust between the ego and the higher self. Trust that admitting a mistake will not result in weeks of debilitating self-abuse and condemnation allows for honesty. Now I experience so much less drama than I used to. My most tender spots are mistakes that mean, according to my ego, I am a bad mother or a petty and unkind person.

Perfectionism keeps a list a mile long of all the times I have not measured up in patience, gentleness, compassion, and grace. My ego desperately wants to be remembered and thought of as a wonderful and loving mother. But beneath the layer of ego is the more genuine desire to authentically *be* loving. Being loving is much harder work than appearing loving, though it is far more fulfilling.

I have to accept and admit when I make the same mistakes time and time again. I have to cultivate the courage to be seen, fully flawed. It sounds so simple! We all know no one is perfect. Why do we keep up the charade of perfection at the expense of our integrity and most intimate relationships? It all comes down to our belief in worthiness. Do we feel worthy in our authentic humanity, or must we strive for worthiness?

Allowing for a dignified path forward makes it infinitely easier to accept the truth and take responsibility for our actions. Saving face can be a saving grace for both ourselves and others. It can be so easy to pass from admitting guilt or a mistake into the territory of shame. Shame is the ultimate secret keeper, and it will not allow the truth to enter the light of day. We simply cannot open our hearts to understanding and growth while we are under shame's attack. Looking deeply and honestly, I do not wish that for myself or anyone else either.

Our culture has given rise to bloodthirsty public shaming rituals rivaling the gladiator games of Rome. Please, for the love of whatever it is you believe you are defending or fighting for, allow for a dignified path forward. There have been countless times—and shall be countless more—when I am in need of redeeming. I imagine if you look honestly within, you may feel the same.

We must not abandon the dignity and sacredness we have given to the self. Otherwise, we become a culture of defensive and offensive people, afraid for our very souls. Harm that has been done to people absolutely needs to be acknowledged. There has been so much abuse to humanity, hidden beneath the stiff outer shell of cultural norms. Yet people who have sinned are still human. There is a difference between accountability and publicly discarding a human life. No one can be lifted out of the fabric of humanity without consequence to the whole.

For myself or a loved one, come what may, I do not wish to stay trapped in guilt, betrayal, victimhood, or blame. I wish to return to authentic innocence, however long that path might take. I believe in reaching for empowerment as it reveals itself. As a mother, I support my children in regaining the full integrity of their essential selves whether they have wronged or been wronged.

Justice is not one of my core values. I'm not sure what a justice system based on love would look like—its main objective being to protect people from harm and restore dignity—but I don't believe any justice system can replace the integrity of wholehearted people acting from love.

Humility Garden

> *"A memory without the emotional charge is called wisdom."*
>
> —JOE DISPENZA
> FROM *BREAKING THE HABIT OF BEING YOURSELF*

Metaphorically, I maintain a humility garden in which I pray compassion, hope, and encouragement bloom for all the days of my life. Imagining planting a tree for my most painful sins feels like redeeming the energy of the painful experience for good. Accepting our mistakes, forgiving ourselves, and making amends becomes a source of compassion and understanding.

Reclaim your innocence and align yourself with your personal sun. Call back the pieces of you that you have left behind, and once again know wholeness. The mere choice to believe in the possibility of your innocence will begin to clear the sludge. You can feel the energy of the hero within begin to shift and reawaken at the promise of once again feeling the warmth of the sun. You are in need of your strength. Your journey is not yet over. You are beloved, and there is work to be done.

Just as the flower responds naturally to the warmth and light of the sun, your essential self responds to the warmth and light of your core values. The eternal values of love, joy, and beauty are all around you and within you when you have the eyes to see them. They are potent, living energies, not just words on a page or lyrics in a song. Living in alignment with your core values, your personal sun, will invigorate you, comfort and encourage you, and guide and nurture you.

This is why the hero/ine's first work is to return to innocence. Innocence is the state where we remember that we can choose to exist in a state of love and joy—where we are worthy of love, and we are made to share love. Innocence is the state where simply being alive is a blessing beyond measure.

If you experience regret or shame over something you have or have not done, said, or thought, it means that you acted against your true values. You have acted *against* your true essential self. The worst of what we have done is not revealing our true selves. We are learning.

Please receive this deeply: the incident causing guilt is illuminating your true values, not defining you by your mistake. When you remove the guilt and once again turn your face toward the sun, you re-experience innocence. You cannot experience absolute goodness any more than you can experience absolute north on the compass.

What if everyone took the pursuit of absolute north so literally that there was a mad rush to the North Pole? What a ruckus that would be. Yet few would argue against the navigational usefulness of the concept of north in human life.

No error can alter the unlimited power of love in human potential. Someone on death row can still cultivate a heart of love. He can choose to treat those around him with love, kindness, and respect. He can share what insights he may have gained from his dark path. He can reach out to others to help them avoid the path of pain. He can communicate his remorse to those he has harmed. He can be an instrument of love and peace in the time he has remaining in this earthly life.

Sirens

When we feel unworthy of divine love and purpose, we may try to fill that need with something else. We try to meet the need for unconditional worthiness on the level we feel worthy of. We may strive to fill the pain of the gaping hole with alcohol, shopping, food, work, sex, or by distracting ourselves on screens. The options for distraction and self-medicating are growing daily. I have come to refer to these as the siren's song from the *Odyssey*. Sirens are magical creatures who know of your personal pain and unmet desires. They may call with one simple melody or compose a more subtle song of harmonious chords to disguise their malicious motives to sabotage your best intentions.

When we hold a painful or guilty story as self, we have a wounded identity in the present. We no longer feel connected to the hero/ines within. Instead of standing tall in our innate nobility, we begin to contract into smaller selves.

We can choose to leave the pain and guilt in the past by healing our identities. We do this by remembering the innocence held within our essential selves. When we find ourselves answering the call of Sirens, there is no benefit from shaming and judging ourselves. This only feeds a vicious cycle. When we engage in behaviors that harm the self, the most important question to ask is, what pain or unmet need are we trying to avoid?

By offering ourselves compassion and encouragement we grow in strength and courage. From the empowered essential self, we are capable of seeing honestly. We can choose to take exquisite care of the self and attend to our authentic needs. With proper application of healing energy, we can regain our innocence.

Our Relationship to the Past

"Memory is an imaginal constellation of past and present that generates a new experience. Memory is not the storing of the past, but the storying of the present."

—LYNDA SEXSON

One of the most essential relationships you have is with your own past. Your past holds the raw material needed to create a fulfilling present and the future of your dreams. This is only true, however, if you allow love to generate your personal mythology. Love can position you in a beneficial and empowered relationship to your past.

I will be completely open with my agenda here. It is my goal to convince you on a cellular level that you are now doing, and have always done, the best you could. I cannot overstate the relief, lightness, and freedom gained from embracing this truth. Allow your innocent self, your full essential self, to reimagine the facts of your past and your current relationship to what now exists in another time and place. Let every label that you do not desire to hold fall away.

There are many powerful stories of inspiring redemption. Many people have generated completely new identities and lives for themselves. They have regenerated a personal mythology with the hard-earned wisdom of their painful pasts. No sin or violation of self from the past can touch the potential to act from love now. We need only to be fully present to our innocent potential in the now.

The past in the hands of fear is a weapon. The past in the hands of love is a divine tool.

The amazing truth is that even after many decades of living with something painful, we can one day turn inward and ask, *Why are you there? I'm sorry I have avoided you. What are you trying to tell me? What do you need?* If you listen, your pain will speak to you.

The return of innocence is what truly makes life feel better—not trying harder, fixing, pushing, doing, or knowing more. When you hold on to guilt or blame, you separate yourself from the unconditional love of the full essential self. Being present with your full essential self simply feels good. It feels abundant, empowered, and loving. It is a paradigm shift from pushing and rejecting to allowing what is natural.

The simple truth is that we would not use guilt and judgment on ourselves and others if we did not deeply believe they were the most effective tools we possess. The fact that we are using these "tools" proves that we are in fear. However, wisdom and the lesson do not reside in guilt. When we shift to trusting love over fear, we transform our states of being.

The difference is as profound as going from pushing your car from the outside in the direction you desire to opening the door, climbing behind the wheel, and driving. Tremendous relief from the pain of guilt and judgment is possible. All it requires is looking deeply into the question of how we best flourish and learn. How do we curate the conditions for our most fulfilling evolution? When you really and truly no longer believe that guilt and judgment are your most effective tools, they will lose their despair-inducing hold on you.

The most comforting and inspiring news I can share is that love, encouragement, and forgiveness are the most effective, most powerful conditions for regaining your personal integrity and maintaining heroic morale. With strong morale and personal integrity, you are empowered to live in accordance with your core ideals. We have to go to this depth if we truly want to heal despair and generate long-lasting fulfillment.

My Root Limiting Belief

Many times I have visited a massage therapist when I experienced tension and pain in my neck and shoulders. At the beginning of the session, I point out the location of concern. Frequently, a gifted massage therapist will locate the source of this tension in a completely different part of my body, often on the opposite side. The layers of muscle crossing one another at opposing angles are chaotic and hard to follow. Yet, as complex as human anatomy is, there is order. We can come to understand our bodies and how the parts work together.

We are equally capable of understanding our belief systems and how our beliefs work together. Through many years of self-reflection and healing, I was able to trace the twists and turns of many of my own limiting beliefs. Many times I felt lost and overwhelmed in my own mind—still unable to connect my known beliefs to the state of being I always returned to.

Then one day, I stumbled upon my most painful belief in a song lyric, laid bare in simple melody. This root belief had been covered up with many other deeply painful beliefs, but none cut to the bone quite like this one. No belief separated me from my own worthiness like believing *I am a burden.* Belief in being a burden is a complete absence of worthiness.

Humans are incredibly complex beings requiring constant care to meet authentic needs. If you do not believe in your own fundamental value as a human being it is easy to come to the conclusion that your own needs are a burden.

The beliefs that no one wants to hear me sing, I'm bad with money, I'm a bad mother, I'm selfish, I'm lazy, and I'm a bad wife all served to cover the unbearable belief that *I am a burden.* Revealing this belief took a lot of patience, love, and the development of inner personal safety. But when I was ready to receive it, the belief revealed itself. As I sat at my piano practicing the song "Silence" by Khalid and Marshmello, my life changed. My breath caught and ancient tears instantly streamed down my face. My most fundamental fear-based belief had been operating completely beneath my own awareness.

I was so grateful for this discovery! My life made complete sense in the light of it. This belief had been the source of a silent, continuous spring of guilt and shame. The belief in being a burden had lain between my essential self and my experience of the world. This belief was the filter that tinged nearly every relationship in my life with guilt. The belief that I was a burden was a constant drain on my morale. By the time the belief that

I was a burden revealed itself to me, I was completely ready to see and release it—though I cried daily for weeks as I let it go. Some part of my essential self knew when I was ready to see and dissolve this belief.

With time, I came to understand that holding the belief that I was a burden was experienced as a threat to my physical safety. If you believe you are a burden, you have the sense that you could be lifted right out of the fabric of humanity. The hidden belief of being a burden was the most potent fear I have known in my life. When living with fundamental fear, it is exquisitely difficult to achieve the kind of internal or external safety required for honesty and authenticity.

In a contracted and defensive posture, we are unable to access innocence, worthiness, or the divine resources of the full essential self. We stay in this posture when we do not trust what is within and therefore try to hide, contain, and control it. Reaching an understanding of what we have been trying to do is where we are empowered to make a powerful choice. Do we choose to remain trapped in a vicious cycle of fear or begin to initiate a virtuous cycle of love?

I recognized that if something is unlovable about my essential self, my soul, then there must be something unlovable about all of humanity. I knew through my love for my children and family that this is not true. However we come to it—by loving ourselves, our children, a partner, or our parents—we understand that if any human is worthy of love, respect, and honor, then all humans are worthy.

Opening ourselves to love means recognizing that divine beauty resides within each of us. Our work becomes honoring and encouraging the expression of divine beauty. If we are living in a sea of miracles, an ocean of oneness, love is always within and without, above and below. Love is the truth and reality of everyone and everything.

The painful belief that I was a burden had been blocking love and abundance for as long as I could remember. It had blocked my confidence in my sacred work and voice since I was a little girl. Removing this barrier released a tremendous amount of creative energy and love. The flow of love elevated the quality of every relationship in my life. My writing and music began to flow at another level. The new beliefs that I have something valuable to give to the world and that my life has meaning and purpose were finally able to take hold.

WORTHINESS

Worthiness does not come from wholeness; our sense of wholeness comes from worthiness. We do not need to earn worthiness by achieving any measure of external success, fitness or beauty standard, financial standing, or relationship status. Worthiness is the fundamental belief required for well-being, not the other way around. To experience a state of wholeness, we have to build our lives around the fundamental right and duty of taking care of our full selves.

Many forces can lead us away from this most essential practice. The one thing all of these forces share in common is a belief in scarcity and not-enoughness. If we truly feel worthy, what could make us trade our innate worth and our natural joy of living for guilt, shame, and despair?

Mental health concerns from addiction, depression, anxiety, loneliness, and grief all may be playing a role beneath what can be seen. Teasing out the relationship of these conditions to personal mythology is extremely difficult. It is heartbreaking how there is still less stigma around purely biological explanations of suffering than around mental health issues.

For my own children enduring difficult times, I wish for them to be as authentically empowered as possible. I would want them to fully embrace their creative power over their beliefs and mythology. To the extent that their interior belief systems play a role in their suffering, I believe these can be explored and healed with focus and time. I also wish for them to explore physical, emotional, psychological, financial, and environmental approaches to well-being. The foundational beliefs that we are worthy of love, joy, and abundance serve to encourage us to get the support we need to thrive.

The self can feel split between being and doing, between accepting self and striving for more, between rest and work, between the needs of the self and the needs of the whole. The functioning of the body depends upon the health and functioning of the cells and equally vice versa. There is complexity and gray area to be navigated. Our morale is our living vital sign. Listening to the vital feedback of morale helps us to determine when enough is enough. For our efforts to be sustainable, we must take morale into consideration.

The way we experience life is dependent upon how we choose to value life. Meaning if we see life as a burden, we are likely to treat it as a burden, thereby experiencing life as a burden. Your needs as a human being can easily be seen as a burden to both self and others through this way of thinking. If we believe life to be a sacred experience, a blessing, we must treat it as such. We have to choose to honor our bodies, minds, spirits, and essential resources.

The underlying goal of this book is to help you elevate your morale by elevating the value of life and self to the level of sacredness. Nothing can be more powerful in sustaining morale as the belief that self, others, and life as a whole are holy. When we hold this belief and treat self and others as holy, we will experience self and life as holy.

This is where we lay the struggle of earning worthiness to rest. Life is not and never has been about your worthiness. Life is about what you are creating. The question is not whether you are worthy of love. The question is, are you being love? Are you expressing and creating love? The noble cell is worthy of life because it is alive. You are worthy of love and have purpose because you are alive.

Your life is your divine invitation, your body the holy ticket to this divine masquerade ball. You don't have to strive to belong or be worthy of the sweetness of life. You are here.

Loneliness

Most of us experience profound loneliness at some point in our lives. The loneliest period of my life so far was the year leading up to nursing school. My first degree was in psychology, so I did not have many of the prerequisite courses I needed for nursing. Most of my friends had moved on after college, and I spent a lot of time alone during this time of my life. I felt like I was in between lives. I was enrolled in a heavy load of courses, including chemistry, microbiology, and anatomy and physiology. This period of immersion into the study of life had a profound effect on me. The cell and its need for a wall to maintain an interior environment became a beautiful metaphor for my own experience.

Though being isolated in our own bodies and our own consciousness can feel painful, this is a fundamental condition for the experience of life. We are composed of trillions of cells and a ceaseless interplay between mind, body, and spirit, yet we can feel lonely because this interior world is held within one consciousness, one unified, creative, and ever-evolving being—the self. It has to be this way for intention, experience, and creative expression to exist. We have to experience this apparent separation to receive the gift of intimacy.

Each of us is a package of divine consciousness and energy. Time and space—reality as we know it—is the medium for personal and collective creation. We are not meant to be alone but designed to build and play with the energy of all of life. Just as in the relationship of the cell to the body, there is honor and dignity in the individual and honor and dignity in the whole of humanity. We simply need to reveal this reality with intention.

SAFETY AND HONESTY

Safety is the condition where your worthiness will not be called into question. Where whatever you reveal cannot alter your worth in your own eyes or in the eyes of another. Safety is another name for unconditional love. Wherever we do not have safety, we cannot have pure honesty. When we don't have self-honesty, we are not fully empowered.

We are afraid to reveal the deepest parts of ourselves because we genuinely believe that beneath the struggle and drama, the story of guilt and brokenness, we are hideous, unworthy of love, and broken beyond repair. These painful beliefs are the result of living in the vicious cycle of shame and guilt.

The truth is when you reach rock bottom and you have faced the greatest fears of your story written in the hand of guilt, the story will begin to dissolve into the nothingness that it is. As the guilty self-image begins to fall away, the light of your true self—your essential self—will burst through. As beautiful as this miracle is to experience, there is a second and simultaneous miracle to behold as well. If this is the truth of your being, this is the truth of all beings.

Geese and Trust

My family has six beautiful geese on our farmette. Three of the geese we rescued, and three we raised from one-week-old goslings. The three rescue geese have not yet come to trust us in the way the geese we raised do. While the three younger geese enjoy eating straight out of my hand, the older geese are too anxious or distrustful to do so.

Out of my love and consideration for the rescue geese, I toss their food on the ground for them to feel comfortable eating the pellets. I have often contemplated how much happier the younger geese are to eat the abundant clean pellets out of my hand. They are able to stand comfortably as I place the pellets at just the right height for them. They genuinely seem to enjoy the closeness as I rub under their beaks and gaze at them adoringly.

I love our rescue goose Arthur very much and would love to share the same closeness and abundance with him. I place his pellets on the ground only because of the distance and distrust that he places between us. I know he is more comfortable scrounging for his pellets on the ground, so that is where I place them. Yet I also hold space and hope that he will grow in trust with time. I wonder if this is how it is with God and us.

PERFECTIONISM

I never thought I could be a perfectionist because I wasn't good at anything and I had frizzy hair. Talk about hiding in plain sight.

Whenever I heard or read about people suffering from perfectionism, I would think with a snide chuckle, *Well, that's one problem I certainly don't have.* I never even gave the idea a second thought. I had a picture of what perfectionism looked like, and it didn't look like me. Smooth hair, perfect dinner parties, immaculate houses, and overachieving were other defining qualities of the perfectionist. I definitely thought you had to at least be good at *something* to be striving for perfection. Truth be told, I didn't believe I was even worthy of the word.

Like many moments of revelation, I remember the time and place when I realized I suffered from a raging, undiagnosed case of perfectionism. I was sitting at my kitchen island reading a book about creative rituals when I came to a section on artists and perfectionism. My perfectionism was so deep, I hadn't even seen it. I was saturated with the need for perfection. *It* was the reason I didn't feel like I was good at anything. I was struck.

My initial thought was, *Oh, God, not another problem to overcome!* However, discovering my perfectionism was an epiphany for me. Somehow all the tendrils of this tendency lit up in every area of my life. I could equally see both its influence and the toxic effects it carried.

One area I could see it most clearly was in my desire to be and be seen as a "perfect mother." It showed up most intensely there because that was what I cared most deeply about. If I wanted the best for my family, how could I settle for anything less than perfection? How could I draw a line that says, "This is good enough"?

When I finally recognized my perfectionism I could taste its flavor and knew instantly it was not love. Honestly, having a perfect mother would be a curse! How could we learn to love and embrace ourselves as human beings without positive examples of humility? Epiphanies are gifts of a virtuous cycle. The work you put into identifying and understanding how love and fear feel keeps folding back into your sacred work.

LOVE LETTER TO THE HERO/INE

The process of transferring fundamental trust from fear to love is far more arduous than it may seem. It truly is heroic work. I have come to recognize this process described in the writings and stories of others. It is always described as difficult and full of doubt. The timeframe for paradigm shift is usually two to three years. This has also been the case for me. I share this not to intimidate or scare you, but to encourage you to honor yourself and the great work before you. Furthermore, I share this to reassure you that trusting and relying on love does get easier.

> The letter below is addressed to Beloved because my greatest wish is that you receive the love you need when you most need it. That is when you are most convinced that you are not worthy of it. Wherever I am, I send you love, faith, and encouragement to carry on.

Dear Beloved,

I am writing this letter from a place of disappointment in myself. So many times I must face that I have made a mistake. I have not acted out of love, as I desire more than anything. The voice in me is strong that wishes to blame another. *This shouldn't be so hard. I'm so over this struggle.* This voice is fighting for the need to feel "right." Yet I know this voice is not understanding my greater need to feel innocence. At this moment, I am out of innocence; I feel guilt. I am choosing to turn from the sun because it illuminates my errors, my pettiness and smallness. How can I believe I am doing the best I can when I can so clearly see a better way? It is deeply uncomfortable, but my trust is growing. I must turn this guilt over to love. The circle of love, beauty, and kindness is large enough to contain the whole of me and my Beloved. I do not need to weave a tale of drama for how I have faltered from my stated desire to live in love. It is quicker and more loving to simply drop the drama. I do not need to be perfect to be worthy. My good intentions are still here to guide me. I have come to this place many times, and I may return to guilt over and over. Yet my faith is growing. It is safe to reveal my truth to myself. The part of me that resides in unconditional love will receive me and give me the courage to turn back to the sun. I am releasing this guilt because I know it does not truly serve me or my Beloved. The way of love is love. I choose to return to patience and kindness.

What do I need to do to heal this situation? What does my Beloved need from me to heal this situation? This is my sacred work at this moment.

Always and forever,
Yours

DESPAIR

I do not wish to turn away from the painful reality of despair. So many people are living in a state of despair at this time. I have known despair intimately. If you are currently in despair, I hope my words will meet you where you are.

I know that you have tried all you know to try. Hope and promise, good intentions, and honest effort have given way to hopelessness. Frustration has led to anger, to guilt, to discouragement, and, ultimately, to despair. You want to lay down the fight, because you no longer feel equal to it. All that you once thought was useful now feels futile. You have brought your knowledge, heart, effort, and energy to bear, and it has not seemed to make a difference. I have been there too. I would be honored to hold the truth of your worthiness and your faith in life until you are once again strong enough to carry them on your own.

I can tell you I lived through a time where it seemed all the lights were out. When we feel that we are tired of life, I believe we are tired of carrying pain and cannot see a way to free ourselves from it. The idea of cultivating morale is not that you will feel the same fatigue and despair you do now and carry on doing even more. The idea is that you will feel better. Much, much better.

There is a phenomenon in human memory that our current emotional state influences the memories we most easily retrieve. It seems a cruel trick that when we are sad or hopeless, all of the memories from times we have felt like this before stand poised for fluid recall. We are left unable to connect with all the times in our lives that we have known joy, love, safety, faith, or a sense of accomplishment. The theory behind memory retrieval bias is that your experiences during past times of stress or fear may be useful to you now.

When I was in my deepest despair, I scraped the bottom of my being, the darkest corners where I was certain the true, contemptible ugliness of myself lived and bred beyond control. To my profound astonishment, brilliant beams of light pierced through the very structure of being. The matrix of the Divine revealed itself. I could see love surrounding me, suspending me, and composing me. In the end I found relief where I most feared to look, within myself.

Within the alchemy of human intimacy in the form of flesh and bone, emotion, imagination, mind, heart, and spirit I was reunited with the Divine. I experienced a rebirth of the awareness of the great Divine. The marriage of the grand beauty and the grand suffering revealed itself.

I had the sense I was literally standing up from living on all fours. In an instant, the recognition of how much greater I was than all my problems startled me. Maybe we are upright for a reason. Our arms are literally and symbolically free to reach for the heavens. What if reason married to faith creates solid ground to stand upon and a wide open sky to reach toward?

To stop growing, to stop reaching for the sun, is death. This is as true for the seedling as for us. The seedling thrives as long as its essential needs are met and conditions are conducive to growth. What this says to me is that we are naturally innocent. Something is interfering when we are not thriving.

When the pleasures on the surface of life fade, we must go deeper to find the nourishment we need to sustain morale. Our personal mythologies dictate what resources we believe are available to us. Much like the belief that what is in your neighbor's bank account is not available to you but what is in your account is, you must believe that these resources are for you.

Awareness of your own true resources becomes more critical during hard times. The usual sources of our meaning, strength, and joy may not be accessible. The questions become, *What now? I have built my life around something that has vanished. What can carry me through this loss and pain? What can hold me and steady me when I have become disoriented? What can I hold on to?* These are the times when morale becomes our primary sacred work.

Embrace whatever metaphor or narrative most supports you through dark times. What imagery holds the most inspiration and meaning for you? What image most fully captures the process you are enduring? What metaphor allows you to see through the pain you are enduring to the other side? What imagery helps you generate morale?

As the source of your vital force, your essential self also holds the key to your most potent power. Regaining access to your vital force and power is what saves you from despair. I am going to share honestly how hard it can be to discover, accept, and love your authentic essential self and how long it can take to find your way back home. It takes tremendous bravery and patience. You have to muster all your available courage and wisdom. You have to cultivate and sustain the morale of a hero. I wish I could offer an easier solution to despair.

I hate to think of you in pain. Asking you to hold on, be patient. Yet it only makes sense that the solution we seek must reach the level that needs healing and relief. A spiritual pain seeks a spiritual salve. Knowing what you are seeking is, in itself, a tremendous bit of progress, though.

I know you were made for this. You were made for life. I dare say that even when you are feeling powerless, remembering your true power will save you.

You are worthy of the sweetness of life. Reach for whatever support and inspiration is available to you today. You are not alone. Help is available. Seek healing and nourishment for your mind, body, and spirit—in whatever ways you can.

"What you seek is seeking you."

—RUMI

RETURN TO INNOCENCE

If you can believe in the power of innocence on an intellectual level, you begin the virtuous cycle of transferring your trust to love. With patient practice in your life, you will begin to feel innocence bloom in your heart and body and soul. Reconnecting to or remembering your innocence will raise the vibration of your entire experience of life. You will naturally see and believe in the innocence of others. You may begin to see the Divine more clearly everywhere you look. You may begin to see your family or circle of friends as a beautiful collection of innocent souls.

There is a powerful relationship between worthiness and innocence. There is immeasurable relief in trusting your nature and relaxing into your natural unfolding.

Innocence is quite simply being in the state most conducive to your well-being, where there are no roadblocks or dams of guilt or unworthiness to alter your course or discourage you. You are beautiful and free. You are serving the whole through your own thriving. There is tremendous joy in this.

The goal of this work is to gain absolute clarity that what is born new, in every single moment, is pure potential. Once this potential is freed from the shackles of the past, it is available to use in whatever direction you wish. You are living in a state of innocence.

SECTION IV
becoming empowered

THE SECOND GOLDEN STRAND OF MORALE IS REMEMBERING that you are powerful. The power contained within every human being is incalculable. We cannot even begin to imagine a world in which every human being is whole and fully empowered. There are many shining examples of what human potential looks like, though. If one human is capable of achieving a state of wholeness and empowerment, then we all possess the same potential. First, we need to believe this is possible for us. Worthiness, potential, and a path to empowerment must be written into our personal and collective mythologies. Morale soars when we know and feel that we are working for something meaningful.

Being empowered is essential for confidence; therefore, it is essential for cultivating morale.

To own the truth of how much of our mythology is fiction and reclaim the creative power of imagination is the beginning of empowerment. The way we choose to use our imaginations to create meaning from the facts of our lives is how we create change. As we become ever more empowered, we are more willing to take responsibility for our thoughts, emotions, and actions. This is because we have embraced the fact that these are where our power lies.

When we choose to create from the laws of love, we return to our true home—innocence. In innocence, we are no longer focused on creating worthiness. We have shifted to creating *from* worthiness. If we make a mistake or fail to understand something, we know it is within our power to respond differently in the present moment. Clear of limiting beliefs and story, we are empowered to create from infinite possibility. This state is empowerment.

We are living in extraordinary times. Empowerment is possible on a level never before known to humanity. However, the challenges we face are equal to the opportunities. This is because the same potential exists for the expression of love as it does for fear. Technology and the global dissemination of information are tools that can be used for the benefit or harm of humanity. We are facing the decision to align the great potential of humanity with love or face dire consequences of war and planetary changes. Remember, for the empowered, the assessment phase (looking at the facts) is just the beginning.

There is no question that while we are extremely powerful, we are not all-powerful. We must acknowledge and make peace with the fact that we are coauthors of our own lives. Our lives are entangled with the lives of many other souls, sometimes in known ways, more often in mysterious ways.

Not only are our lives impacted by other beings exercising their own power and freedom around us, but many people feel that God, life, destiny, or fate is also coauthoring our lives in meaningful ways. I believe that the relationship we hold with coauthors is of great importance to understand. If you hold the belief that these powers are scary, evil, or even indifferent, you will live your life in a state of never-ending defense.

Defenses are fear in action. Defenses protect something precious, sacred, until we have become empowered enough to hold the truth. Our empowerment is the process by which we come to possess the wisdom, gentleness, courage, strength, and faith to truly release our defenses. Empowerment has to hold our vulnerability.

What is your relationship with that which is beyond your control? Can you trust a force outside yourself enough to be focused on the development of your own power? How do you reconcile what you have influence and control over and what you do not?

THE TRUTH ABOUT MAGIC WANDS

The magic wand provides a flawless metaphor for empowerment. The wand itself serves as a directed funnel of personal energy. It is held in the hand, demonstrating that it is a direct extension of one's personal power. Empowerment in the most basic sense stems from the ability to focus attention on what one *does* want while directing one's energy to what one has control over.

The narrow barrel of the magic wand concentrates the energy of the user into a narrow stream of laser focus in the desired direction. The user then recites a spell stating the exact desired outcome, the intention. The result is a visual display of the marriage of the intentional focus of one's mind, energy, and body in the direction of what one wishes to achieve, while being fully present in one's own sphere of influence.

The successful wizard is not focused on what he does not want, who is not helping, or the idea that things shouldn't be the way they are. In other words, there is no drama. The wizard is crystal clear and self-possessed. The result of drama is far more similar to a Fourth of July sparkler—energy flying off in every direction in a brief, though spectacular, display of wasted energy. The image of the wand serves to visualize the intentional flow of directed energy. Every aspect of the wizard's mental, physical, energetic, and spiritual self is brought to bear in alignment and is, therefore, extraordinarily potent.

It cannot be denied that being in command of one's focus has become more challenging in modern life. Focus and attention have become commodified. Since being empowered requires that we have command of our attention, we must meet the challenge of reclaiming sovereignty over our focus.

Challenge of Scope in Modern Life

In modern life, we have a greater understanding of the whole world than in any other period of history. As is typical of cultural evolution, change brings with it both gifts and challenges. How do we handle being exposed to the challenges of the whole world in real time? Attempting to hold and address everything at once leaves individuals disempowered and demoralized.

Most of us are familiar with a feeling of hopelessness in response to challenges that are beyond our personal spheres to solve. How do we spend as little time as possible in this disempowered state? How do we mobilize our vast resources of information, ingenuity, and deepened understanding of our interconnectedness of life to respond with intention?

Finding approaches to living that sustain the morale of both individuals and communities benefits us all. This is the way to create an effective, intentional, and sustainable effort in the direction of desired progress. The more important our causes, the more important it is to approach our challenges with wisdom and intention and the less time we want to lose in overwhelm, blame, and despair. What can be done now and today? How can we begin a virtuous cycle leading us to a brighter future? What systems do we need to create to ensure steady progress?

GIFTS OF TIME

Perhaps eternity lacked the intimacy God craved.

When God first hung the stars and planets in the black velvet universe and wound the great celestial clock, time was born. The holy gifts of order, contrast, rhythm, and divine cycles were bestowed.

Our world was gifted night and day and the majesty of earthly seasons. God created beautiful nesting containers within linear time. Reliable, visible, sensual packages of time to be opened with love and gratitude. The sense of nesting results from the fact that all of creation is one, just cleverly disguised in packages. I like to imagine God designing the packages of time we enjoy here on Earth, creating years, months, days, and nights with which to create and experience life. Time is sacred.

Units of time can be seen as units of creation. The greatest gift of time is perpetual newness. Time is the river that flows across the veil in constant movement. Time is not a dark shadow waiting to overtake you. It is an element, a medium of expression and creation. Time is the father who sets his child down in the meadow and says, "Play, beloved." The mastery of time hinges on seeing, feeling, and believing in the gift of eternal innocence.

The Day Is King

Of all the packages of time, I find the day to be king. If you can master the day, you are golden. A package of a day creates a scope that allows for intimacy and intention. The day provides the visual promise of a beginning and an end, a sacred hygge circle made precious by its impermanence. A day is a mini life, exquisitely ripe in the now, yet possessing enough space to create, work, play, and rest. One earthly rotation, one spin of the celestial dance of which we are partners. A day's portion of work, rest, nourishment, celebration, and grace is the most we ever need.

When love resides within our personal seat of power, we can finally be fully present to the day. We have released the guilt, regret, and anger from the past. We have cultivated trust and faith in ourselves for the future. Today reveals itself as the gift it truly is, the present. This makes the day feel like it is suspended in a beautiful string of pearls. There is peace with the past, faith in the future, and the gift of presence in the present.

All the elements you wish to experience in your life must be present in your days. The full essential self longs to express itself and be nourished in the day. You honor the self by setting time for joy, time for sacred work, time for loved ones. You must allow time for rest and movement, dining and celebration, prayer and communion with the Divine. Hearty morale requires receiving the nourishment of the day.

When fear is in your personal seat of power, you will feel like there is not enough time for all this. Fear, with its focus on safety and scarcity, will work very hard to convince you to put off the fruits of a love-driven life until later.

Interestingly, fear will allow for numbing comforts. Without the genuine joy and pleasures of living a love-based life, you may feel compelled to "turn off" at the end of the day. Alcohol in excess, mind-numbing entertainment, and shopping all serve to dull many of the feelings of anxiety and disappointment associated with the fear-driven life.

Most people spend time and energy daily in self-medication. This explains why you might always find time for endless social media scrolling or television but not time for reading in the hammock, doing creative work, or gardening. Love wishes to enhance the experience of life, while fear seeks to numb the pain of missing out on life.

Daily Portion of Work

When we are not clear about our day's portion of work, we will not be satisfied by what we have accomplished. Without definition, work stretches out before us in an unbroken and relentless line of to-dos and lack of fulfillment. It is of vital importance to morale to gain clarity on a loving portion of work that moves you in the direction you desire. Defining the day's work allows you to know and *feel* when you have completed your daily portion of work.

Much has already been written about the importance of journaling and a morning routine. I would not be writing this book or living the beautiful life I enjoy without these essential practices. Remaining in the energy of love requires continual assessment. *Do I need to shift my expectations around timelines or how much I can get done to honor my morale? Is my body communicating that I need time for rest, movement, hydration, nourishment?* My journal is one of the most powerful ways I explore these questions. Journaling allows me to identify and work through resistance to the plans for the day. My journal is a place to explore and envision dreams. Finally, it is a place to let residual, gnawing emotions fall upon the page. The distance created allows me to gather the concerns, intuition, and wisdom my words hold while releasing the draining energy.

Completion is the fulfillment of engagement with the sacred work of life. We crave completion on the daily level as much as on the quarterly, yearly, and full-project levels. The feelings of empowerment and pride are deeply nourishing to morale and are what fuels the virtuous cycle. Thirty days of completing your daily portion of work with pride feels infinitely better than thirty days of not-enoughness. You also will accomplish more in thirty days of working in a state of self-possession and empowerment. Allow yourself to play with this idea. When you are in a state of worthiness—of love—what you can reasonably, cheerfully accomplish in a day is enough.

The energy you apply to gaining clarity on the work before you in the day is the work of becoming empowered. When the work you accomplish within the day is connected to your core values and grander vision for your life, you experience high morale.

This can be true even through difficult times, but you must consciously make the choice to see and experience enoughness. Mastery of focus is the single most important task of empowerment because energy follows focus. The voice of the ego and others around you likely will need to be reassured when you shift your focus to rest, connection, and play. The well-being of the full essential self requires that we focus on the full experience of life—not just work and goals. The gifts of the full essential self will far exceed what the ego or work alone can give. What we choose to focus on in the day determines our morale and our quality of life. This is what the choice to live in love looks like on the daily level.

The scope of the day's portion of work needs to fit into the framework of your actual life. Learning what you can accomplish within the range of high morale requires wisdom, discipline, and practice. We spend time and energy in physical, emotional, social, and mental work that we often do not account for. After many years of working with this principle, I still struggle to balance the varied needs of the full essential self. My ego remains convinced I should be working a little harder and I should be a little further along. Nonetheless, there is grace and solace in holding the loving intention to honor my morale. The practice has made a slow but steady transformation of my energetic state. I am filled with compassion and gratitude when I read my own journals from even a few years ago. Living within the harshness of my own judgment and the constant guilt of not being enough was excruciatingly painful. Even my ego is now convinced that living within the paradigm of love is a much better place to be.

When days are full of commitments, bringing our focus to where we are can take more effort. Yet how often are you engaged in a simple activity such as driving or washing dishes, but your focus remains engaged with pushing, stress, and not-enoughness? The energy, presence, and joy lost in this way is not productive or useful.

Quiet and seemingly unimportant activities can be infused with sacredness and pleasure when we bring our focus to what we are doing. For example, in a full day, bringing our focus and full essential self to the ritual of a cup of tea can provide the break and nourishment we need for a boost in morale.

As simple as this sounds, paring down our expectations can be extremely difficult. This is because we have to choose to release seemingly valuable outcomes and let go of excess. Fear lives in scarcity, so it is reluctant to do this. Fear does not want us to get too comfortable, to feel like we are doing *enough*.

In order to set expectations with wisdom and intention, we have to become clear on two things. Firstly, within the context of the day, choosing to spend one's time and energy on one thing means those resources are not available for other things. Holding ten priorities in one's attention and focus does not mean that we are actually tending to ten things at once. Quite the contrary, we are likely neglecting ten things at once. Only you know when you are applying sufficient focus, time, and energy to do what you set out to do and feel that your resources have been put to good work.

Secondly, to set expectations with wisdom, we must understand what matters most to the self. Does your experience of life, your morale, matter more than pushing to do more? Is a 10 percent tidier house worth a drop in your morale? The clearer we make the choices before us, the more empowered we are to make wise choices.

Learning to trust the natural evolution of self through love over fear-driven drive takes practice. Practice is another way to describe the process of transferring trust to love. It takes a tremendous amount of love to trust that what you accomplish in a day is enough. This is especially true when you embark upon a long journey, like writing a book, or when you don't have clarity on when a project will end. In fear, we seek clarity and certainty. For example, not truly knowing if or when I will finish this book triggers impatience and the desire to push. Managing this fear is part of my daily portion of work.

Hearty morale is the vital sign that you are trusting in love and is therefore your greatest asset in assessing and designing your days. Morale is strong when we believe we are aligned with what we want to create. This means you trust that what you are doing now is creating what you desire. You are facing your personal sun and receiving its nourishment now, in the day.

Honoring the day has become my single most important act of self-care. I intentionally cultivate trust that I have enough time, inspiration, energy, and focus for my work and patience to handle the challenges of the day before me. I have made a practice of releasing frustration, failures, conflicts, and disappointments through daily morning journaling. This practice allows me to face the day with a freshness that fills the day with creativity, wonder, joy, and grace. The more I honor the day, the richer my life feels.

Fear would have you believe that time is a thief, always running away with your precious moments and opportunities, never offering you the chance to catch up. But the beauty of time, seen through the lens of love, is that time carries you onward. The sun sets and rises with you and beckons you to begin anew.

Weeks, Months, Seasons, and Years

Bigger goals that require more time and effort to accomplish still can be organized lovingly into larger containers of time. Weeks, months, and seasons of the year are perfect for spreading out sacred work in a way that allows for sustainable morale and fulfilling accomplishments.

The goal is that each container of time allows for both the enjoyment of life and progressing through our goals and personal evolutions. As we transfer our trust to living and working within the paradigm of love, this balance becomes easier to find.

My family and I celebrate a quarterly Celebration Leisure Day, or CLD for short. Rest and celebration are very effective for interrupting fear-based drive—the mounting sense that we will never get enough done. CLD is a day we plan for months in advance and do our best to keep completely free of engagements. Sometimes we celebrate big accomplishments or progress on our home restoration. Other times we celebrate the end of the school year. In quarters where my husband and I feel like there's nothing significant to celebrate, we work to reset our mindsets. Surely we are all worthy of a day of leisure and celebrating life on a quarterly basis.

Chronos and Kairos

Chronos, or linear time, is a gift of the veil. It says, "Here, now." So much of human desire, longing, pleasure, and pain are born of linear time. Time allows for intimacy because it is a container for focus. We can savor the experience of following individual notes of a melody or the presence of a beloved. It is sweet heaven to experience this cup of coffee, on this porch, in this season, in this moment. God is with me and enjoying this beauty through me.

Nonetheless, I believe we still have the ability to transcend earthly time. Linear time does not alter Kairos, or eternity; it merely covers it.

For many years I felt as though I was skimming across the top of my life like a pebble skipping across water. Living in a chronic state of fear creates hurry and distrust. In a loving state, there is safety and trust to expand, relax into time. Time feels so much fuller and richer when you drop down into it, beneath the peaks and valleys of the surface.

Beneath the surface is where we reside in our fuller selves. We are able to observe more clearly all that the ego is working so hard to hold together. We are better able to support the ego from the abundance and creativity that lie just beneath the bustle and stresses of the everyday. From this place, it is easier to dip into creative energy—the energy required for writing or composing music, for example.

We can drop even further still to the calm water beneath the waves. This is where we experience kairos. I have found much of the resistance to sitting down to write comes from the discomfort of the sudden shift from hustle and bustle to receptive creative flow.

When people refer to being in flow, I imagine underwater currents of time. Beneath the surface of chronos, the relentless tick, ticking away subsides as another dimension of time opens up. Children inhabit kairos until we train them to follow the tick tock, tick tock of the clock. These currents seem to flow between dimensions, and I believe we are able to communicate more freely with the Divine in this realm. The voices here have a unique quality that you can begin to recognize in your intuition, inspiration, and dreams. Kairos is home to imagination, creativity, muses, angels, spirits, and God. Faith is the key that unlocks the depth of time.

Through passing time in kairos, we can strengthen our connection to the Divine and our higher selves. We can bring spaciousness to time. Life is so much richer and more fulfilling when we answer our soul's call to enter the magical realm of kairos.

Enough, Good Enough, Soon Enough

The simple mantra "enough, good enough, soon enough" releases three types of scarcity—quantity, quality, and time. When you choose to recognize that you are enough, good enough, soon enough in the present moment, you release yourself from scarcity. Whatever state you are in at the present moment is your current reality. Judgment does not alter reality; it alters only your perception of reality. Using the power of imagination against self—to see lack and deficiency—limits access to the resources that are actually available to you. We do this only when we believe scarcity or withholding love and approval will somehow motivate or protect us. Choosing to see yourself and your evolving circumstances as enough is seeing through the lens of love. Recall that only love provides nourishment and possibility.

Fulfillment comes from the feeling of enough, good enough, soon enough. The feeling of enoughness originates from how we see ourselves. The filter of our self-worth colors how we see our work, relationships, health, body, environment, finances, and so forth. Are you enough, good enough, soon enough?

Look honestly. Is there a benefit to believing that you are not enough or not good enough? Is there truly a need for hurry if you trust you are on the path to what you want? What are you placing above your fundamental right to enjoy your life? What is more important than savoring life and expressing your essential self? If your life is exhausting with little pleasure in your days, the fuel behind your actions is not coming from love. You are not so much moving toward what you want as moving away from what you don't want. This sometimes subtle shift in perspective is at the heart of empowerment.

Take debt, for example. Let's say you desire to live in the freedom, peace, and joy of abundance. Currently you have a certain dollar amount of debt. When you empower yourself with awareness about your finances, you can create a plan to free yourself from the debt in a given amount of time. Once you have made the plan and begin to follow it to the best of your ability, you are free to focus your resources on other things. Once you achieve clarity and you are doing what is currently within your power, additional resources consumed on your debt issue are wasted.

Just as the cell always expends energy, tending to its internal environment, ever reaching for a balance that can never last. This is the condition of life. When we are in the safe and abundant state of enoughness, we are truly available to the beauty and joy of life. Our morale soars.

Movement and Navigation

To be alive means we are always in motion. Our labeling of good and bad, love and fear, stems from the basic drive to move away from pain and toward pleasure. We seek orientation in our desire to express ourselves in the world. The greater our trust in ourselves and the world, the greater our ability to navigate a more nuanced universe.

As we gain in self-possession and trust in ultimate reality, we are able to comfortably live in a colorful world and move beyond black-and-white thinking. Freedom and potential also require space for and acceptance of uncertainty. To be free, to experience freedom, we have to learn to trust both ourselves and the world we are navigating. We gain confidence in our ability to handle the risks of moving toward that which we desire. This is the land of butterflies in our bellies, doubt, and insecurity.

Overwhelm

In the absence of self-confidence, courage, and self-trust, overwhelm can feel like a more comfortable place to hang out. It took me many years to unravel my payoff for living in a state of overwhelm. I simply didn't yet have the confidence and self-trust to live freely. Situations and circumstances outside myself truly felt completely overwhelming. This misperception came from my habit of living contracted, trying to stay safe by staying small. In hindsight, from a more empowered state, I can clearly see that I have always been more powerful than the circumstances and challenges I have faced.

ESSENTIAL ENERGY

Your essential energy cannot be created or destroyed. You possess all the energy you need to create the beautiful life of your dreams. If it does not seem this way, your energy is simply being misdirected and bound up where it cannot be put to good use. Our belief systems act as conduits that release, move, contain, or waste energy. We literally can use our own power and resources to limit our true potential. As human beings, our energy is expressed through and contained within our physical bodies.

As discussed before, our belief systems determine whether or not we trust the energy and nature of life. Not trusting our own nature results in distrust of our innate power. This lack of trust will be written into beliefs that aim to limit our power and therefore keep us safe.

Understanding this concept is the beginning of becoming empowered. Building a relationship of genuine trust with our own power and that of the great coauthor may take time. As we gain access to more of our essential resources through trust, we are better able to care for ourselves and others. We are able to engage in sacred work on another level.

The idea of living well can feel so exhausting—all the work, cooking, cleaning, workouts, and emotional management stretching out endlessly before you. It can feel like you couldn't possibly keep it all up. It is amazing how much vital energy you can consume in drama and staying contracted.

If you follow the idea that energy can neither be created nor destroyed, what is happening to all of our tremendous energy? It is being turned in, compacted, medicated, and denied. We also see its explosive power in the world, but not always from a place of deep love and wholeness. We see it exploding out in anger and violence and numbed in apathy. Sigmund Freud described depression as the result of anger turned inward. I believe this to be true. When the social price of expressing our anger is deemed too high, we turn it in. We take the poison. We become toxic. Then we numb the resulting pain as best we can.

Let's use abundance as an example for working with essential energy. In a fear state, you are trying to move away from scarcity and some flavor of not-enoughness. You are reacting to what seems large and more powerful than you. In other words, you are not focused on what you desire and what is within your control; you are focused on scarcity. Being focused on scarcity means that you are residing in the energy of fear. Fear cannot provide resources or nourishment. It can only deplete. Over enough time, this approach to abundance will lead to fatigue, discouragement, and, eventually, despair.

If, on the other hand, you are focused on abundance and what you do want, you are in a creative state. You are not merely reacting to your environment; you are inspired to create something new. The inspiration this orientation creates, coupled with the focus on whatever is within your control, equals empowerment. However long it takes to create what you desire is the time it takes to transform your beliefs, thoughts, and habits to align with abundance. There truly is no hurry. Hurry itself is scarcity energy.

The Golden Crayon

I like to simplify the concept of personal energy with the imagery of crayons. If you want to create a picture of a verdant green forest, you have to use a green crayon. We would not expect to use a purple crayon to create a green forest.

This is exactly how energy works. For me, the energy of abundance is peaceful, fun, and full of ease and luxurious time. Let's say this energy has a golden color. I cannot push, rush, stress, or make my way to this state with any other energy than abundance. I must color with the golden crayon to create a golden picture.

Even if you manage to use scarcity to manipulate a certain external circumstance into being, it simply won't feel like love and abundance. You can't color gold with a purple crayon. This metaphor is oversimplified in the sense that our unique, personal energies are in constant movement and contain varied emotions. Nonetheless, the clarity of this simple metaphor is tremendously helpful. The image of the golden crayon can quickly shift your energetic state.

If the feeling you desire is not thriving in your life today, it will not appear magically tomorrow. When this law of creation is truly received on the heart and soul level, you will experience a rush of gratitude unparalleled. You no longer have to wait to feel what you want to feel. In fact, you believe on the deepest level that embodying this beautiful energy now is the most effective, practical, and straightforward means to accomplish everything! If you have not yet felt the rush of relief and gratitude, you likely still hold greater belief in fear. That's okay. You don't have to force the process or pretend you believe what you don't. A steady transfer of trust is a beautiful way to go.

On Resistance

Resistance in life is like gravity. It is essential for expressing intention in the world. Without the gravity on our planet, we would not be able to stand or exercise physical control of our bodies. Our bodies have developed in the presence of gravity in order to work *with* gravity.

Anyone who has seen the movie *Gravity* with Sandra Bullock remembers the scene where Sandra is spinning uncontrollably and indefinitely into space. She has nothing to hold on to or press against to stop, orient, or redirect herself. It is truly terrifying. We may just find a little more acceptance of resistance—perhaps even gratitude—when we think of it this way.

Learning to discern the difference between the effort required to accomplish something and the unnecessary resistance created through drama is necessary for efficiency and efficacy. Mastering resistance is essential for intentional creation and empowerment. Resistance is a necessary part of human life; nonetheless, resistance can feel exhausting.

The idea that resistance will always be between you and whatever it is you desire can have a negative impact on morale when you let it. The truth is we can manage our resistance effectively and efficiently when we remove drama and have clear, personally meaningful goals. The resistance that I have to overcome each time I sit down to write this book is a perfect example. The more I build up the resistance in my mind, the less likely I am to actually sit down and write. *I don't want to write today. This is so hard. I'll never finish this book.*

It helps me to remember the task of a single writing session has a set amount of resistance. I have to overcome only the resistance to sit down today, not all the resistance of completing the whole book. Seen within the scope of my day's work, the resistance is manageable. Especially when balanced with a solid dose of pride for showing up to do my best work, regardless of the outcome of the writing session. When we are mindful to balance the day's portion of work with joyful and rejuvenating activities, we experience cheer. To experience this balance in our doing and being, we must remain in our innate worthiness. In a state of worthiness, we remember that how we feel and our state of morale matters.

For a wonderful in-depth discussion of resistance as it relates to art, I wholeheartedly recommend *The War of Art* by Steven Pressfield.

A powerful exercise for working with resistance is to visualize that which is applying pressure and its relationship to where the pressure is being applied. Does it make practical sense? Are both ends of this equation depleting you? Are you encouraging movement toward what you desire, or are you using your own energy and power to further defeat, belittle, or trap yourself?

To illustrate this principle, I will use my lifelong desire to play piano. I used to judge myself harshly for not practicing piano. I believed if I wasn't such a procrastinator or so lazy, I would already be playing piano. This method of speaking to myself stemmed from a belief that if I was hard enough on myself, I would eventually get better results. However, in this example, I was placing pressure on myself using guilt and shame. The reality is that in order to show up at the piano, I simply needed to overcome natural resistance—another form of pressure. How could adding to the load I had to overcome be a useful strategy? That is like adding a mound of heavy bricks to a load you are already unable to lift.

If you are using your own resources to defeat yourself, you are on the road to discouragement and despair. We cannot guilt or coerce ourselves into doing many important things, especially for the long term. For anything we want to sustain over time, we must take morale into consideration. If the joy and pride have left an endeavor, the bird has flown from the cage. We were not intended to be slaves to life. Life does not need to feel like a burden.

DRAMA

Drama is the use of imagination to make anything we want to accomplish, feel, experience, or accept more difficult. Sources of drama include making something personal, arguing with reality, and judging self or others. The ultimate source of drama is attaching worthiness to anything. When we attach our own worthiness to any relationship, goal, or external condition, the situation becomes exponentially more difficult, muddy, and draining.

There is a reward for everything we do. For drama, the payoffs include distraction, denial of personal responsibility, and perception of safety. When we are afraid of something at a higher level, we can utilize drama to create overwhelm at a lower level. For example, fear of facing a difficult relationship could manifest as drama and overwhelm around housework. The drama and overwhelm are unpleasant but not as uncomfortable as turning one's full attention to the difficult relationship.

Avoidance, overwhelm, and drama have distinct energetic signatures that you can learn to recognize. Take the challenge of staying current with laundry in a busy season, for example. Completing laundry requires honoring the task for its important role and planning time in your schedule. Doing laundry is not actually difficult. Once drama becomes attached to the task, however, you will recognize a circuitous spiraling of thought. *I will never catch up. I'm so exhausted. This is all too much.* Feelings of inadequacy or hopelessness may result from circuitous thoughts that feel out of your control.

The feelings and thoughts of overwhelm are the same no matter what goal you are working toward. You may discover once your housework is running smoothly you find there is drama around submitting a manuscript or establishing a new health practice.

The common theme is that you actually are empowered in the situation once you gain clarity and intention. Drama serves to excuse us from the work of moving forward. What I know is that energy, time, focus, and emotion lost in drama are not available for creation. Drama drains our confidence and therefore negatively impacts morale.

Training yourself to recognize the "feeling" of being in a state of drama and intentionally turning your focus back to where your power lies is possible. You must ask yourself: *What is it I want? What is my highest priority at this moment? What is presently within my control to move me in that direction?* The antidote to drama is practicing clarity, elegance, and grace.

DRIVE

Many people go through life in a driven state, attempting to make up for past failures, disappointments, and inadequacies. The unholy drive that is so often responsible for robbing our days and nights of peace and joy is fed by a toxic cocktail of regret, disappointment, dread, fear, and shame. The pain of living in a driven state motivates much of our self-sabotaging behaviors.

I never thought I would be free from the drive. Then one sunny day, I realized I was running from the *story* of all my miserable disappointments. Separating one's essential self from "the story" by any perceivable distance, regardless of how subtle it may be, is a miracle. The choice to free oneself from the story becomes immediately evident.

Without the story of my procrastination or laziness, what would keep me from showing up at my piano or at my computer to write these very words? Drive is fear's attempt to motivate and control. Love motivates with inspiration, moving toward what feels good and what brings joy. Fear attempts to motivate by moving away from what is painful and depriving the self of joy. Fear has a no-holds-barred approach to motivation. Through mixing up your signature cocktail of guilt, shame, anger, and regret, fear is constantly coloring in vivid pictures of worst-case scenarios.

The freight train I used to board at dawn to the shriek of the whistle, straight through to my nightly crash, is gone. Not a soul around me misses the roar of those engines. Letting go of the need to earn worthiness has revealed a new life.

Right Pressure

Every task or goal requires a set amount of effort to accomplish. Any extra effort in the form of time, energy, focus, or emotion can be considered wasted. Frequently this excess effort is destructive to peace of mind and relationships.

Imagine waking up and applying ten or a hundred times the effort and pressure required for everything you do. Every movement you make with your body, every step you take, you expend many times the effort required. You pick up your coffee cup with a hundred times the force required. When you speak, you say everything with a hundred times the force and assertiveness required to communicate your message. Every challenge you face, you spend a hundred times the focus and emotional energy required to resolve it. Throughout the day, tension, stiffness, and fatigue would build.

Now imagine you have done this for a year. Stiffness would lead to decreased range of motion and pain. Ease, fluidity, and grace would be completely lost. How often do you waste your own essential resources in this manner?

Fear would have us forever vigilant, pushing against all perceived and potential threats. Yet, if we believe that fear holds the secret to our safety and power, this is how we go through life. How much effort is actually required to accomplish what you need and want to do? What could you do with all of the energy and focus currently wasted in drama?

Adding drama to the practice of clearing drama is obviously not efficient either. We all use our imaginations and energy to create drama. When you are transforming your state of being to love, your state of being will feel like love today. You will have patience with yourself and others. Decide to feel enough, good enough, and soon enough once you have set your intention. Trust the power of the virtuous cycle.

A word of advice: if you intend to complete a task that you are resisting, try to schedule this task for the morning. The resistance you feel is likely to drain your essential resources until the task is completed. Once the task is completed, you likely will experience a rush of pride and a corresponding lift in morale. This lift will help energize you while bringing confidence and joy to all the other tasks in your day.

Honoring All That We Are Doing

When we seek to understand our morale, understanding and honoring all that we currently are doing is critical. It is easy to become so focused on achieving goals that we discount all of the routine work we do to maintain our lives and relationships. Evaluating the following areas of life can illuminate how much we are truly accomplishing and managing:

- Care of full essential self: physical, mental, spiritual, soulful, and emotional

- Responsibilities of work or career

- Care of children

- Care of all intimate and personal relationships

- Care of physical home

- Management of finances

- Engagement with personal growth

- Advancement of personal goals and dreams

Challenges or periods of intense growth in any of these key areas require immense essential resources. The less we judge our current energy levels and morale, the better we are able to understand them. The better we understand our morale, the more effectively and efficiently we can respond with intention.

When we have particular goals in mind, we tend to dismiss all that we accomplish outside of our goals. We can feel we have not accomplished anything at all when it is more accurate to say we have not progressed on a particular goal as much as we had hoped.

Honoring every effort made and every step forward, no matter how small, feeds our pride, endurance, and perseverance. Looking at every step backward as a learning opportunity builds resilience and wisdom. Viewing our lives and goals from a holistic perspective grants us a more realistic and compassionate viewpoint.

Most goals require us to move beyond our current level of functioning—beyond our comfort zones. Managing uncertainty, doubt, and stress depletes our essential resources of focus, optimism, and energy. When we are dealing with issues that leave us feeling vulnerable or exposed, we must allow for extra comfort, reassurance, and time.

This is also true for healing. Whether we are healing physically, mentally, or emotionally, we require significant resources of time and energy. Others around us may be completely unaware of what we are going through internally. We may be the only ones to provide ourselves with the needed grace, patience, kindness, and exquisite self-care that we require. During periods of heartache, mourning, and life-altering events, caring for our morale can become our highest priority.

Love does not judge morale; love seeks to understand and care for our morale. When we are patient and kind, we frequently find that we have not been taking all we are currently facing into consideration when we set our goals and expectations.

Yet there are also times when we feel down and cannot understand the source of our suffering. This is when we must practice kindness and patience the most. We must actively choose to listen to the needs of the self and remain open to inspiration and guidance.

The ultimate goal of morale is to engage in virtuous cycles. Within the virtuous cycle, we feel confident that when we stay committed to what we are doing, we are moving toward what we want to experience and create. Residing in the energy of love is the only way to engage in a virtuous cycle. Even when we are unsure of how to proceed, we can choose to stay in love by practicing patience and kindness. By seeking understanding and remaining open to inspiration, we will eventually find our path forward.

Monitoring Progress Along the Way

Recognizing and celebrating progress—creating a system for recording and reflecting on the progress we make on our goals—is essential for sustaining morale. The knowledge that what we are doing is moving us toward what we desire brings confidence and joy to our sacred work.

It is natural to move our attention very quickly from one task or goal to the next once the first goal is completed. This is actually beneficial because we are most empowered when our focus is engaged in the present moment. However, when you become frustrated by the difficulty or amount of time a current project is taking, you can refresh your morale by recalling all the progress you have made along your life journey. Keeping a journal is a fantastic way to revisit the mindset and challenges you faced and overcame in the past.

On the other hand, you may reflect on your progress honestly and believe that you have been "stuck" for a long time. This is an invitation to evaluate whether or not you are engaged in a vicious cycle. If it becomes clear to you that you are, the best way forward is to intentionally return to a state of empowerment. From there you can release limiting story and drama and align your energy with a virtuous cycle.

HARNESSING THE POWER OF IMAGINATION

Art is the act of creating something new from what is.

Imagination is a solid and dependable source of power. Imagination is translingual—it is the language of divine consciousness. Imagination is not bound by the limitations of time and physical reality. Imagination sees value where all seems lost and broken because it is not limited to the purely physical-temporal realm. It can see straight through fear, pain, and sorrow to the golden potential within our human experience.

As an artist, imagery is everything to me. My soul speaks to me in metaphors. Imagery, colors, words, movies, music, and lyrics all have the power to communicate to the full essential self. All of these mediums provide a means of moving and containing personal energy. We can use this movement of energy to create something new from what currently exists.

There is great power contained in words. Ancient words carry potent energy. It is also important to remember that language is alive and constantly evolving. Language adapts to meet the needs of a culture and expresses the hearts of its people in real time. Seek the words that serve you in creating what you desire, and if they don't yet exist, create new words. You can create a word that expresses anything you feel you are or any emotion you experience. The fresh interpretation of all through art keeps wisdom alive.

To harness the immense power of imagination, we have to be aware of how we currently are moving, expressing, and storing our own personal energy in words and imagery. We can develop a kind of intelligence in the way we use our imaginations.

On Labels and Diagnoses

When we accept a label or diagnosis, it becomes a part of our personal mythology. In the hands of love, labels can provide understanding, validation, self compassion, and community. A label or diagnosis can help us honor the challenges we are facing and get the support we need to overcome them. In the hands of fear, however, labels can be used to judge, belittle, isolate, and place limitations on the self.

Our mythology determines what a label or diagnosis means to us. Our mythology will also determine what resources and support are available to us. We want to use the power of our imaginations with intention to create a mythology that honors the full essential self and opens us to receive all the care we need to thrive in mind, body, and spirit. We are the ones who decide when and for how long a label serves the self.

Metaphorical Intelligence

Metaphors compare two seemingly distinct concepts with the aim of revealing or understanding a shared essence. They are used because they reveal something new or provide insight into a previously known concept by transferring wisdom, understanding, logic, essence, or experience. Metaphors provide a bridge between understanding physical and spiritual aspects of self.

Metaphors reveal a language the mind, heart, body, and soul all can deeply understand and respond to. A common language that provides a means for the miracle of personal harmony. Wholeness is to feel the harmony of mind, body, soul, and spirit as one.

The richest metaphors reflect the creative intelligence underlying all that is—the signature of the Divine. A metaphor can reveal the beautiful logic that simultaneously explains the movements of my grandmother's clock, the changing of the seasons, and the movement of the planets in our solar system.

This same logic illuminates the mechanics of my personal being, the changing of my own seasons, and the orbits of the many souls in my personal, intimate universe. Anytime "as within, so without" or "as above, so below" applies, there is a suggestion of a deeper, universal truth.

Metaphors highlight existing definitions and illuminate the underlying relationships between constructs in our lives. In the process, they highlight limitations or provide templates of wholeness and well-being. Metaphors serve as crystal clear mirrors, because they provide enough distance for objectivity.

The highest form of metaphor carries a universal truth with the signature of the divine.

Plants and animals allow us to see the integrity of living without drama, the inexhaustible beauty of the unique, personal expression of the Divine.

The images and metaphors we use reveal our personal mythologies. Clichés we have heard and cling to and metaphors we reference seem so innocuous on the surface. They seem to not actually be revealing anything about us personally. Therefore, we feel safe in revealing them. If you are holding and using these images, however, without question, they do reveal a lot about you. Are you in a battle, on a journey, or playing a game? Are you a disciple, a knight, or an athlete? Are you a victim or a hero?

Similar to narrative intelligence, you can develop metaphorical intelligence. The etymology of the word metaphor is to carry over or across. At the time I discovered these etymological origins, I was still captivated by the idea of the chasm between love and fear. The image of the great chasm was paramount in my mind. The idea of the metaphor carrying me across the great chasm was powerful and offered tremendous relief at the time; it was a way forward. I was then able to navigate successfully in the direction of where I wanted to go by adopting metaphors, images, and clichés with intention.

Metaphors are capable of delivering epiphanies.

As you sift through the imagery and wisdom contained within your own mythology, keep the following questions in mind.

1. Is this image a whole or partial metaphor? Does this image or metaphor apply to the whole of life or isolated circumstances? Does it hold meaningful answers to any of the ultimate questions?

2. Is this metaphor from the perspective of love or fear? What does it say about innocence and guilt, for example? Safety, trust, abundance, and faith?

What does this metaphor reveal about my relationship to empowerment? Does it reveal a way forward? Would I choose to believe this metaphor reveals the ultimate truth? Do I want to keep it close to my heart? Make it part of my own personal mythology?

Metaphors are extremely useful for identifying drama. We say someone's heart is broken, but this is a partial metaphor. As an entity of energy, the metaphysical heart cannot be broken. Yet the metaphor retains meaning as it honors the pain someone is experiencing. It implies "a wounding" requiring care and rest and time to heal. The problem arises when people take the metaphor too literally, believing their hearts are, in fact, "broken." I believe a great many of us walk around living life from a belief of brokenness.

AUDACITY

Audacity is the vulnerability of authenticity, supported by worthiness and courage.

When I was a little girl, I used to sing full out, all of the time. There was only joy and self-expression, no judgment, in my singing. I distinctly recall the day that changed for me. It was a hot summer day, and I had been in my room belting out my favorite tunes to my portable stereo. My favorites at the time were Whitney Houston,

Aretha Franklin, and Cyndi Lauper. When my dog Luke started barking in the yard, I went to the back porch to let him inside.

When I stepped outside, I could hear my music playing through my open window. It was loud—as loud as if I were in my own room. I realized with a wave of nauseating shame and humiliation that any passerby could have heard me singing. I was mortified by the idea of my unguarded voice being heard. Who was I to sing like that? Who was I to burden someone with my voice?

I was around the age of twelve the first time I experienced shame around being heard. I still recall the sensation of shrinking within myself out of fear of judgment. I wanted to protect myself. The feeling of smallness can often be mistaken for safety.

The belief that my voice is a burden has not fully left me to this day. Clearing this belief, this block to my ability to sing full out in front of people, remains a part of my sacred work. It's astounding how much of sacred work is invisible. Each of us is engaged in hard work that can be understood and appreciated only from the inside, work that requires the morale of the hero/ine to persevere through and overcome.

Much of this invisible work is managing and confronting vulnerability, uncertainty, and self-doubt. It is fundamentally creating interior safety for the self in what feels, at times, like a dangerous world. Interior work requires self-acknowledgment for the resources of energy and time it consumes. In order to generate the courage and strength required to express our essential selves, we must value the path.

LOVING EXPECTATIONS

Expectation is a story. Our own expectations are always operating whether we are aware of them or not. We are constantly comparing what is with what we think should be. Our expectations determine whether we feel defeat or pride, enoughness or scarcity, hope or despair, safety or fear. Expectations play a critical role in determining when we are in a vicious or virtuous cycle. Expectations are created through imagination.

The Gap

Between your current reality and that which you wish to create is a gap. This gap is where all the magic of intentional creation happens. The gap is the space required for freedom and creative potential. As rich with potential as the gap is, moving into the gap can be exquisitely painful. It is full of uncertainty, doubt, and vulnerability.

What matters most is what we place between our ideals and our perception of our current reality—how we fill the gap. When our expectations are coming from a place of fear, they likely are attempting to protect us from something we do not want to happen versus leading us toward something we are creating. From this place, the expectations we place on both ourselves and others are harsh and unkind because they are generated from fear.

Loving expectations are patient and kind, and they provide the real possibility of fulfillment. Loving expectations feel like enoughness, gratitude, and pride in ourselves and others. Loving expectations come from a compassionate understanding of where we authentically are and where we are evolving to. Loving expectations are essential for maintaining healthy morale.

The bottom line is this. You have to commit to shifting your expectations until you are left with a positive emotional balance. A sense of pride, joy, accomplishment, celebration, or gratitude will carry every one of your intentions further than the weight of defeat or despair.

In other words, at the end of the day, you want to feel good about your day's work, yourself, and life. That is what the choice to live in enoughness feels like. With practice, this "lift" will be with you when you go to bed and when you wake up. It will blossom and grow in your life.

Explaining how we can become so deeply attached to beliefs that are ineffective, disabling, and depleting is difficult. How does it take so long to recognize that our limiting beliefs simply do not work? Yet, there it is. Limiting beliefs are born of fear, and as such can be healed with a steady and consistent application of love. For many decades of my life, I was deeply entrenched in belief in pressure, pain, and guilt as primary instruments of personal power.

We can actively choose to live in awareness of our morale and remain in virtuous cycles. As with all paradigm shifts, there is an inevitable period of transition.

Blessings and Burdens

Blessings can easily become burdens, and burdens can be seen as blessings. It all comes down to the energy in which we hold our circumstances. The blessing of our homes can become burdensome when we treat the work of homecare as a burden. The work of homecare can feel like a blessing when we remember the blessing of our home. Relationships can feel like burdens when, through fear of loss, we try to control them. The love we feel for a loved one can become a burden when we focus on loss.

In order to sustain morale, we have to receive the nourishment of the blessings in our lives. The comfort of our homes, the beauty of nature, the extraordinary gift of imagination, and the miracle of our bodies are all gifts we can receive without noticing. Gratitude is a beautiful place to begin working with the power of your focus. Love sees beauty and perfection in our circumstances. Love sees souls within our loved ones.

What is beautiful about the way things are? What is the gift, the possible message in what is?

KNOW THY FEAR RESPONSE: FIGHT, FLIGHT, OR FREEZE

Knowing your subconscious habitual response to fear is essential for empowerment. Your mind and body have been conditioned and have developed an automatic response to the perception of a threat. Your fear response is written into your beliefs and biochemistry.

A whole cascade of chemical and physiological changes occur the instant you perceive a loss of safety. The same response occurs whether the perceived threat is emotional, social, or physical. Come to recognize how this process feels in your body, thoughts, and emotions. There is so much valuable information to be gained by recognizing what is happening in real time or even afterward upon reflection.

Release any judgment around the presence of fear so that you can receive its message. What you find threatening is likely not actual physical safety but something that holds meaning within your personal mythology. Do you fear loss of identity or power? Are essential relationships or your connection to the grand design being threatened? Is there a perception that you are moving outside the light of your personal sun and thereby losing direction, nourishment, and meaning? Do you fear not being right or losing innocence?

When looking at your history with fear, you likely will find a pattern. For me, my initial response is to freeze. The feelings of being stuck, powerless, and hopeless are a direct result of this relationship to fear. I'm afraid of freezing on stage. I try to freeze my joy and potential, afraid of somehow ruining or losing what I most value if it is exposed.

In intimate relationships, I am deeply uncomfortable fighting. Pain and shame are immediate and debilitating when I experience anger. I much prefer to close down, to freeze. It feels safer. I tell myself I am keeping myself from using harmful words that I cannot take back. But I am pouting, withholding, and protecting my own sense of rightness. I am being petty and small. I know the freezing is no less painful or harmful for my beloved or myself than fighting or fleeing. Somewhere along my life, I learned that freezing was the safest response.

When I recognize this pattern emerging in myself, I have to choose to bring unconditional love to these situations. I say "choose" because it is not yet my first response when fear is present. When I choose to imagine myself and my beloved in a field of love, I can then begin to see the situation from the perspective of love. This allows me to see with compassion and clarity the choices available.

It is all too easy to pass on patterns of fear to our children and play them out indefinitely with those closest to us. My active and ongoing practice now is to first calm the scared part of myself. Anger, frustration, and shame are energy moving through us; they do not diminish our self-worth or empowerment. When I am able to remember this, I eliminate drama and am able to move toward a loving state more quickly.

From here, I gain perspective and seek to remember the other available responses to fear I possess, thus regaining empowerment and alignment with my core values. For me personally, I ask, *How can I bring faith, beauty, and joy to this situation?* This is the best way I know of to restore myself and my beloved to a state of innocence.

ALCHEMY AND CRUCIBLES

Life contains inherent struggle, pain, and difficulty. We are each here to evolve, grow, and transform our pain through the practice of aligning with love. Alchemy provides a beautiful and enduring metaphor for bringing meaning to painful experiences. We are not meant to suffer for the sake of suffering. Pressure, pain, doubt, and uncertainty are part of the process by which we learn to embody love. We are meant to endure trials, resistance, and opposition in order to overcome fear and create with intention. Alchemy is the transmutation of everyday toil into spiritual gold.

We can choose to practice responding to the challenges and irritations we face from the energy of love. Through this daily practice, we grow stronger, clearer, and more focused. By choosing to embody love, we are expressing love. We are residing in love. We are expressing the divine nature of love in physical human form. While it requires focus, intention, and reflection at times, residing in the energy of love feels good.

For example, I have the core values of faith, beauty, and joy. I hold the intention of bringing each of these values to all of my relationships and work. Connecting my desire to reside in love to the effort I put into my sacred work is essential for my morale. I recognize the difficulty and effort as being the means by which I create what I want to experience. Without connecting my work to my desired outcome, irritations and challenges appear to be merely obstacles to what I want. Life can very easily begin to feel like a series of exercises in frustration and disappointment.

On Entering the Crucible

When a challenge or trial is long and arduous, we describe it as a crucible. In this trial, we are undergoing pressure and stress as we seek to release fear and emerge transformed on a deep level. Staying committed to our values while enduring difficult conditions requires endurance and sustainable morale.

The process of writing this book has been its own crucible. I committed to the process and began the work with some understanding of the time, focus, and effort that would be required. However, as I made my way through, I encountered fear I could not have anticipated. I faced battles with insecurity, unworthiness, doubt, resistance, impatience, and loathing embedded in the process.

I have done my best to recognize and manage drama, yet it still has been a difficult, long, and sometimes painful process. What makes this experience alchemical is that I have endured the process with intention. From the beginning, the reason behind writing this book was my love for my own children. I wanted to understand how to cultivate my own morale, and I wanted to leave my children the best wisdom I possess for making it through hard times. I was not going to back out of this commitment. Fueled by unconditional love for my family, my fear had finally met its match.

Full of trepidation, but of my own volition, I entered the crucible. I have had to sit with excruciating pain, frustration, insecurity, and anger to stay the course of writing this book. Without judgment or blame, I had to accept where I was. I had to learn to respond to fear with love. Responding in love meant cultivating kindness and patience toward myself to the best of my ability.

In the process, I was releasing what I knew I wanted to release in order to reveal something new. The pain, effort, intention, and energy have been transmuted into personal treasure. Greater confidence, empowerment, faith, joy, and innocence are the gold found within this crucible. I have become more of who I want to be through this process.

I don't know the ultimate meaning behind human alchemy. Our intimate, personal, physical selves are—by design—shrouded from the mystery of the great whole. What I can say is something meaningful is created within the containers of our intimate lives that contributes to the whole.

I believe in something I call emotional entanglements. When I look at the difficulty humans can have releasing painful, heavy, even debilitating emotions, I have wondered why this would be. One of multiple scenarios is that the pain is entangled with something else a person wants to hold on to.

The pain of losing our first love can be entangled with losing the feeling of innocence and optimism. The pain of losing a beloved is tangled with the love we wish to hold on to. How do we release one without the other? How do we purify the love, the optimism, and the innocence and release the pain that feels attached to it? This is the work of alchemy.

I don't believe we would have physical bodies, minds, and emotions if they weren't essential to the alchemy of human life and the Divine. The process of evolution our individual souls undergo is valuable and purposeful. I believe we are cultivating, purifying, and expressing energy in this lifetime. Through the work of our lifetimes we are a creative part of something breathtaking to behold. As we transmute our personal energy into love and joy, we enjoy the fulfillment of experiencing these states.

When we move beyond the level of pain and suffering in life, there is only love, beauty, and awe. There is great joy in remembering to see life from this perspective. Even shrouded in mystery, it is enough for me.

The Alchemy of Family

A family is an alchemical container, containing the essential selves of all its members. Between each family member, there is a relationship that is also a container. Marriage, sibling relationships, and parent-child relationships are each an intimate container for alchemy.

All of these relationships exist on the physical, spiritual, and mental levels. As life is always in movement, relationships call on us to grow, respond, and evolve with time. It is deeply painful when we feel unable to love and be loved by the members of our family.

Like the noble cell, a relationship thrives when it is able to receive nourishing love, maintain a boundary of commitment, and release the wastes that accumulate in the natural processes of life.

All intimate relationships require the work of clearing waste. The accumulation of irritations and misunderstandings become toxic when left too long. When relationships no longer feel open, supportive, and loving, we may begin to close our hearts to try to protect ourselves from pain.

When through vicious cycles a relationship becomes toxic, we face a critical choice. Do we want to end the relationship, continue in a vicious cycle, or begin a virtuous cycle of healing?

Clearing negative energy takes the time it takes. Building trust in a new way of being takes time. Rebuilding trust and faith in relationships requires patience. Eventually, through dedication, commitment, practicing respect, and ongoing forgiveness, we can clear the blocks to our natural love and affection.

Alchemy comes from the heat, struggle, and pain of the quest to return home. We have to release the impurities of guilt and blame to return to innocence.

Through honing the energetic container of the self through clarity and intention, we are changed. Our energy is transmuted. This is how I choose to see the purpose of my life. I am here to use my experiences, internal and external, to make metaphysical gold. Alchemy brings forth the Divine on Earth.

ON LIFE AS A JOURNEY

A common metaphor is that life is a journey. It is undeniable that our conscious experience of life is constantly reinforcing a state of change and movement. As we have explored with the cell, this is part of the physical condition of life. We must continuously move to live. Honoring this reality in metaphor makes a lot of sense as it is very useful most of the time.

The argument against the metaphor of the journey is that we are never at peace, at home. Our attention is eternally turned outward as we seek the next destination. Feeling as though you are eternally waiting in this state—waiting to arrive, waiting for the next "thing" to happen or come into your life—is all too natural. How do we truly embrace the present moment when we are always focused on the destination? How do we find a sense of space, stillness, or abundance in each step of the journey? Surely, we all know on some level that the end of the journey, the destination, is death.

It seems prudent to learn to enjoy our days while we experience the glory that is life. Can we learn to honor the two simultaneous realities that we are on a journey and we are eternally home? Home is where we meet much of our essential self. We have to find a way to turn our attention inward if we want to commune with the higher self or experience the soul's joy of living. In my personal understanding of the essential self, the spirit is always striving for betterment, to evolve into the ideals of love. Meanwhile, the soul seeks to savor the full experience of earthly life. Our physical selves, our egos, are on a journey of a lifetime, always moving forward on the arrow of time. Meanwhile the Divine within us is always still and at home in the realm of mystery.

Exploring and cultivating trust in the eternal resources of our inner worlds is how we can experience a sense of solidity and soothing continuity in our days. The metaphor of the ship at sea is ideal for marrying these two realities.

The myth of the *Odyssey* is a metaphor of archetypal proportions. The ship of Odysseus serves as his temporary home away from home. He remembers his home on land, and his ultimate goal is to return there; however, he must first journey in the space created by linear time. Odysseus's journey allows him to encounter strange lands and characters, thereby encountering varying aspects of himself.

Dead Ends

There are many hard and painful facts in life. Death, broken relationships, trauma, disappointments, and knowledge that we have deeply hurt others, to name a few. I am in no way trying to deny or dismiss the pain of these facts.

I am, however, questioning whether any of these facts is a dead end. As long as we are alive and possess the power of our imaginations, we can choose to move forward in the best way we know how. The passage of time is a continual new beginning. The power of imagery lies in its ability to organize and move energy. Imagination can reveal a way forward or keep one trapped in a broken cycle. Many times a simple shift in focus reveals potential.

Every time we perceive we are victims or have committed sins, we hold on to residual energy until we forgive. This residual energy can be redirected to growth and clarity, or it can be placed as a barrier between the self and personal sun. Holding on to the energy of guilt or blame directly keeps us out of the guiding, healing light of our personal suns, thereby keeping us stuck in purgatory. There is nothing to gain from the time lost in purgatory. We remain there only when we do not believe we are worthy of redemption or we don't know the way out.

As beings of energy, in a universe of divine energy, all dead ends are illusions. In fear, we feel trapped in illusions. The feeling of being trapped in a dead end can seem tragically real nonetheless. In general, the feeling results from being unwilling to release something that is keeping us stuck or resisting something we do not believe we can endure.

Maybe we fear we cannot face the consequences of something we have done. Sometimes we have dear values that seem to be in direct opposition to one another, split energy we don't yet know how to resolve. We may be holding on to something that seems to hold even more value than life itself. Bringing the light of love to these awful, messy, and painful circumstances can be helpful. Unconditional love can help illuminate a path forward, a path of redemption.

Create a circle of safety within yourself. What is the belief that is creating the illusion of a dead end? Possibly *If I admit to this, I am unworthy. If I accept this, then my life will lose meaning. If I give up on this goal or dream, I am a failure.*

Is there any drama you can clear to gain a better understanding of your situation? What is within your power, and what is not? Are you enduring a process that simply requires time and patience to resolve? Here, your choice is to accept where you are now or fight reality. Sometimes you must honor the fact that powers outside yourself are limiting your choices.

All that morale requires is that you honor the fact that you are suffering and reach for what remains in your control—even if all that is in your control is how you choose to relate to the difficulty.

Feeling powerless is painful. To care for the self when we feel trapped, we must clear all drama. All energy invested in resisting the past or current facts is lost to you. Clear drama to see where your power currently lies and allow yourself to move forward from there. Trust that what is within your power at this moment is enough.

Ultimately, the way out of any dead end is to make a decision. Figure out the nature of the decision before you. Is there something you must decide to do, allow, or accept? Take the time to weigh your options. Make the best choice you can with the knowledge you possess. Trust your future self to care for you. Choose the path of love. When you are ready, move forward with courage and intention.

COMFORTING RITUALS FOR MORALE

Following in the wisdom of those who have gone before us, we can engage in nourishing rituals to sustain us. Intentionally setting times in the day to be present and experience the comforts and simple pleasures of life is one way to cultivate morale.

We may set time aside to read a poem with a cup of tea in the afternoon or create a ritual of an evening walk in nature. When we are present and open to the beauty of nature or inspiring words, we remember our deeper selves.

What is comfort? Comfort is the feeling of being embraced in care and acceptance, exactly as we are. In this state of internal safety, we can relax completely into the full measure of our being. We can expand and fill our own authentic space, without constriction or friction. There is no pushing or pulling. To comfort is the act of honoring something within that is worthy of loving care just for being.

Comfort is that which cradles you by yielding itself to your true shape. When we are comforted, we can relax into loving care and support. This is the condition that is required for safety and honesty. The whole world needs an abundance of comfort to face the challenges of our times.

Comfort allows for a deeper state of presence that lies beneath the trivial details of daily life. From this deeper presence, we are able to receive the nourishment and beauty of life. Here we gain access to the wealth within. Comfort reveals the sacred interior garden from which courage and joy bloom.

When we truly believe in the value of something, we will reach for it. We will willingly receive it. We must honor comfort by engaging in comforting rituals to experience its gifts. The simple act of engaging in comforting rituals is the choice to honor our own worthiness.

Comforting rituals restore dignity to life by tending to the soul within. They reaffirm that life is worth living, regardless of our circumstances. When we engage in rituals of comfort, we invite joy and magic into our hours. We create space and the conditions for the full essential self to express itself. Whether we are in tears or laughter, silliness or sorrow, comfort communicates that we are worthy of receiving love and acceptance.

The instinct to comfort children with loving care is so natural. What happens to this natural instinct to offer and receive comfort once we've reached adulthood? It's as though past the time of childhood innocence, we are no longer worthy of protection or cherishing. We must eternally "do" and be strong. Yet in life, strength without soft vulnerability is dry and brittle, lifeless.

The same tender innocence that children possess is still within each of us. This beautiful tenderness is worthy of comfort and protection regardless of the passage of time. In fact, it is the vulnerable part of us that holds so much of what we often feel is lacking—joie de vivre, imagination, audacity, and vigor for life.

Honoring this part of ourselves through rituals of comfort, we re-experience the magic of childhood anew.

The most important feature of whatever rituals you choose is that they are authentically comforting to you. When a ritual is effective, you look forward to it. You complete it feeling richer than you were when you began. It does not feel like one more thing you need to or should do.

Comfort is deeply personal. The less we feel we can afford these small luxuries, the more important they are to prioritize. When we care for our morale, our morale will care for us.

NOTES ON PERSONAL GROWTH

When I was in need of guidance on how to parent from within a loving paradigm, I took a course called Positive Parenting Solutions by Amy McCready. One of the most enlightening concepts was the parent ego state. When we are in the parent ego state, we are correcting and instructing. The course put forth the idea that as parents we don't want to spend more than 30 percent of the time with our children in this state.

The idea is that too much time spent in the parent ego state is fundamentally harmful to the parent-child relationship. Children begin to feel they are not accepted or "good enough." The high ratio of correcting to acceptance degrades the loving relationship.

This concept was an epiphany for me. The exact same principle applies to the relationship we have with ourselves. When we are guiding from a place of love, we are patient and kind because we honor the fact that we are already loveable. We are enough, good enough, soon enough. From this place, we do not feel the need to spend more than 30 percent of our time correcting or pushing ourselves. If we do, this is roughly when we begin to notice our morale and quality of life suffering as well.

You can apply this idea to all the goals you have for yourself. From writing a book, healing your beliefs, or losing weight, you don't want to spend more than 30 percent of your day pushing and correcting your behavior. Morale will suffer because you have moved into the energy of fear. When you are coming from love, there is no need to hurry.

GIFTS OF THE METAPHORICAL FIRING SQUAD

If you were on a path and encountered boulders that impeded your moving forward, you would simply move them or go around. When you encounter "boulders," or obstacles on your authentic path you must do the same. As you work toward a goal, the ego often acts as a firing squad of negativity. The metaphor of the firing squad is so exquisitely useful for identifying the limiting beliefs impeding your path.

I like to think of the firing squad as dictating my semester's curriculum. For example, I once had the thought that I would like to be a singer. The firing squad immediately responded with a barrage of shots aimed at leveling this lofty dream. *What?! You are too old! You don't have any talent! Do you know how many people are pursuing that dream?!* It is amazing how the firing squad will reveal its position and all its ammunition when confronted in this way.

With just a small amount of distance, you can observe these limiting beliefs and list them on a sheet of paper. There is your curriculum. Work with the fiction contained within each of your limiting beliefs. Many times a belief contains a fact surrounded by fictional assumptions. Separate all the fiction from the fact so you are empowered to use your imagination for yourself.

For example, does the fact that I have traveled around the sun forty-five times mean that I cannot sing? Work through each of the limiting beliefs blocking your path in this way. Work at whatever pace allows meaningful progress toward clearing your path. At some point, you placed the beliefs there or allowed them to be placed there, and you can decide to move them. It doesn't really matter who placed these limiting beliefs as they are now impeding your path. Therefore, it is most empowering to take responsibility for identifying and clearing whatever is in your own way.

Pursuing dreams or setting big goals is a sure way to identify limiting beliefs based in fear. Your ego will quickly identify and list each of the limiting beliefs blocking the path to where you want to go.

ON AGE

A common lesson that appears on our curriculum relates to chronological age. In our current Western culture, it is generally acknowledged that we are youth-obsessed. The result of this is the sense that we are somehow going to reach some imaginary expiration date. Alive, yet past the point of being able to express ourselves fully or contribute meaningfully to the world through our creative work. The metaphor of an expiration date generates drama in the form of resistance to aging and scarcity around time.

I recall once doing a classic personal growth exercise where you explore what you would truly love to do by asking yourself, *If you could not fail, if you had no financial or time barriers, what would you pursue?* I allowed myself the time to sit with this question and answer it truthfully. "I would sing" rose quickly to the top of my dreams. Singing feels like a pure expression of my heart and soul. Singing feels like freedom and joy. It is one of my original joys.

When my ego lets go of my voice and I sing from my full essential self, I feel at one with this beautiful, grand world. I thought, *If I didn't have debilitating performance anxiety and couldn't fail, that's what I would do.*

During this exercise, I was sitting in my car in the parking lot of a ballet school, waiting for my kids. My car was filled with sippy cups, and cheddar bunnies carpeted the floor. I glanced in the mirror at my tired face, my hair piled high in a messy mom bun. The evidence that I was in a distinct phase of life with very clear limitations was strong. I remember smirking at my own face and thinking, *That ship has sailed.* I may have even said out loud what a waste of time the exercise was. I had gone deep within, only to reveal an expired dream.

Now, a decade later, I have a much more beautiful metaphor than the ship that sailed without me. It is a gift from the French language. In French, you don't say I *am* an age; you say I *have* a certain number of years. I see a distinction in these two phrases that completely alters my relationship to my own age. First, to say I have something rather than am something creates space. The way I see it, the essential self is at least two-thirds beyond time and space and, therefore, ageless. Yes, the physical body beautifully follows the arch of a human lifespan, but what exactly does that need to mean?

Many of the qualities we unwisely associate with limited stages of life are, in fact, timeless, eternal, and therefore ageless. Joy, beauty, faith, creativity, empowerment, wisdom, peace, vigor, innocence, and so forth. We all have access to wisdom that exists outside of our chronological experience. The young possess tremendous wisdom, courage, and understanding. When we are young and hear this wisdom from within, we may doubt it. Yet upon retrospection, we see that we have always possessed understanding beyond our life experiences.

There is also no expiration date on the spiritual gifts of life as long as we live. I now envision that for each year I have lived, I hold one rose. These decades comprise a beautiful bouquet of roses. Each year is deemed a blessing that continues to add richness and beauty to my life. I *have* these years.

From this abundance, I now feel it is the perfect time for me to share my voice, to write, to sing, to be seen. I have more to share than ever before. Reimagining my age in this way has been tremendously liberating and empowering. Yet the messages against aging are pervasive and strong. As a culture, we are still in the process of liberating ourselves from the limitations of age. At this time, seeing beyond the rigid stereotypes of age is an active practice.

SECTION V

engaging in sacred work

THE THIRD GOLDEN STRAND OF MORALE IS THAT THERE IS sacred work before you now. Sacred work is any work that honors the Divine in you, others, and the world. If you are in a state of despair, working on your morale is your first sacred work. If you are suffering from addiction, recovery and healing are your sacred work. There is no hierarchy of sacred work.

Whether we are called to work on the physical, mental, or spiritual levels, we must be the ones to honor the sacredness of our own work. We also possess the power of supporting and encouraging others by honoring the sacredness of their work.

There is great fulfillment in answering our calling, developing our gifts, and creating our lives in alignment with our authentic selves. All of this requires an active living in the world.

WHERE TO BEGIN

You begin exactly where you are. This is the only place you can truly start your sacred work. Wherever you are, it is the perfect place to start.

There was a time when learning homecare was my sacred work. The overwhelm I brought to housework was robbing myself and my family of the experience of beauty and joy. In order to master the art of homecare, I had to gain greater command of my focus and create clarity of what a well-kept home looks like for us. I had to develop loving expectations for myself and my family. I had to build confidence in my ability to consistently bring that vision to reality.

I learned what it felt like when I tried to care for my home in the energy of fear versus caring from the energy of love. I had to learn how to cultivate the feeling that what I did was enough, good enough, and soon enough. All this work was really about learning to cultivate my morale. Within the realm of housework, I learned to engage with sacred work cheerfully and confidently.

That very same self-mastery was then available to begin writing this book, another form of sacred work. I would not have been able to write this book before I gained greater control over my focus and confidence in my ability to show up consistently for my work with intention.

When I was suffering from despair, my sacred work was cultivating my own morale, though I did not recognize that at the time.

There is always dignity in sacred work, whatever form it takes. This is so because dignity and sacredness are inseparable from life. Remembering to honor the dignity of our work is the beginning of cultivating morale.

In dignity and integrity, we recognize the fundamental value of life. Healing from addiction, caring for ourselves through hard times and mourning, restoring our integrity after we have sinned, and healing relationships are all sacred work. Now, my sacred work includes caring for my family and our home while writing this book and creating music.

I recognize that throughout my life, my sacred work will shift and evolve with me. Cultivating morale always will be my first priority because, at its heart, sacred work is that which moves us into love. Sacred work cares for your essential self, others, the world, and God simultaneously. It is all one.

CONNECTING TO OUR CORE VALUES

By embracing our own values, we affirm that we are worthy vessels of whatever is most important to us. In the collective whole, we have champions for justice, beauty, health, compassion, peace, truth, and service.

Core values stem from absolutes and are filtered through the unique filters that are "us." Through our personal filters, we can choose unique purposes that are fulfilling to us. For example, the absolute value of justice could be filtered through an individual and result in a calling to work with juvenile delinquents.

You are the one who assigns value and sacredness to life, yourself, and others. How often are you valuing lesser things than your worthiness and happiness? Can you see how you are trading your unconditional state of worthiness for the idea of attaining a goal? Or withholding your feeling of worthiness until you measure up in some way or another? Why would we do this? How do we straighten out our priorities? We do this by embodying our core values with our creative energy, time, and focus.

What is difficult about simply doing this? Let's take the value of beauty as an example. If we don't feel worthy of residing in beauty in mind, body, and soul, we may choose to chase beauty on the physical plane. We obsess over outward beauty because that is what we feel worthy of. In fear, we do not trust that our true beauty is enough. We may not feel we deserve to feel beautiful on the emotional, mental, soul, or spiritual level.

When we finally recognize that seeking beauty only on the physical level is unfulfilling, we may choose to welcome beauty on the soul and spiritual levels. We can begin to seek beauty everywhere we look. We can choose to reside in beauty. Little by little we infuse more and more of our focus and creative energy into the full meaning of the values we seek. We are engaging our full essential selves with our core values.

We literally expand the circle of beauty until we are fully within it. For me, true beauty is the sense or essence of the divine shining through physical reality. True beauty is not diminished by time; it is revealed in time. The recognition of the marriage between divine and human is where true beauty is seen and fundamental worthiness becomes apparent. We can seek it in the aisles of department stores or in gyms, but we will not find what our full self needs. On the deepest level, we are seeking to remember the Divine within. We feel beautiful when we are in a state of worthiness and when we are honoring the sacredness of life.

Each of us expresses and serves our own core values in a unique way. With a fundamental level of respect and civility, these differences can serve the whole of humanity. This is brilliant on a scale I cannot help but believe is divine.

If something inspires you, you are worthy of it. If one of your core values is beauty, and you place yourself outside the circle of beauty, you will suffer greatly. You may turn your face away in shame and sadness from that which could nurture and sustain you in your time of need.

For example, let's say you have a personal core value of truth. If you are holding on to a time when you were dishonest, you place guilt between you and your personal sun. Through life, you may acquire enough of this unprocessed guilt that it becomes painful to think about honesty and truth. You essentially place yourself outside the nurturing circle of light that truth provides. Sacred work always involves honoring and expressing our core values.

ORIGINAL JOY

I was born singing. When I was a little girl of six or seven, I wrote my first song. It was a love song to my mom. My heart expanded and filled to overflowing when my family found joy in my song. Somehow, my family has kept this song alive for all these years. The lyrics and simple melody, first held in memory, were then lovingly recorded by my dad when I was nine.

I remember basking in the glow of the love I had expressed and shared. I was still an audacious little girl. Decades passed between my first song and the time I began writing songs for my first album. The purpose of all work with mythology and learning to follow the true and steady compass of morale is to return home.

Authentic joy does not have an expiration date, and it does not rely upon external validation or success. Thousands of songbirds live in the trees around my home. They sing because they are alive. They sing in joy, to attract their mates and call to their babies. They do not need permission to be songbirds; they simply are.

ON WAITING TO BE CHOSEN

I am an artist, but I have not always embraced this simple truth.

For most of my life, I have not felt worthy of the word. Worse still, I have not seen its significance in designing my life. Yet not understanding one's nature does not alter it. It is quite possible to neglect and abuse one's essential nature for decades and still it remains. When I think back upon the audacious little girl I once was, it is difficult to trace the circles that led me deeper and deeper into a scared and contracted state.

Being an artist feels like something you have to be chosen for, and I never felt chosen to be an artist. In reality, you are the one who does this choosing. You choose this for yourself. You choose to see the value in the time and energy spent pursuing your art. You choose to value and safeguard your creations.

Before I started writing songs and playing piano, I was locked in a fear paradigm. I believe I had always recognized on some level that my music was sacred work. Interestingly, the sense that the work was sacred actually kept me from doing anything at all. If the work was important and sacred, it surely had to be very good. I wanted it to be excellent.

I wanted to sing and play the piano beautifully. I wanted to express myself authentically in my own songs, and I wanted to feel proud of my songs. The problem was that excellence was not an option for me yet. I had to embrace the opposite of being excellent—being a novice. The work became releasing all judgment surrounding being a novice. I had to release the belief that I was too old to be getting started. I had to release the idea that if I sang and it wasn't perfect, it meant that I wasn't really a singer after all.

My simple and transformational epiphany came from Julia Cameron's book *The Artist's Way*. She said, "If something is worth doing, it's worth doing badly." This completely revolutionary idea liberated me from my self-created dead end.

As soon as I allowed myself to embrace the beauty of being a novice, I was freed to get to work. Now I love being green! I find so much joy and freedom in allowing myself to be where I truly am. I am so proud of simply showing up for the daily work. Choose to be proud of the work that is before you now. The work will evolve with you.

For me, my art is not about the approval of others, money, or fame. It is about granting myself permission to experience the joy of music and self-expression. What could possibly stand in the way of choosing this for myself? Unworthiness is the great barrier to all the love, joy, and abundance that we all already possess. Worthiness allows us to find value in our own self-expression.

HUMILITY AND THE FULL ESSENTIAL SELF

Sacred work can be seen as the process of becoming self-possessed. As we care for the needs of the full essential self, the self will begin to share its authentic desires and divinely given gifts. These gifts are meant to be developed and shared with the world.

As we become empowered, we will inevitably face limiting beliefs around false humility. We live in a culture that predominantly encourages people to stay small. When fear is our dominant paradigm, we are ever guarding against empowerment because we fundamentally don't trust human nature. We are taught to be fearful of the extraordinary power we possess because we don't trust it. The result is shaming individuals who are growing a little too big for their britches or making others around them feel uncomfortable.

Here's the thing: we cannot inspire the courage of others to embody and express their full essential selves if we are afraid to do the same.

In the love paradigm, there is no hierarchy. One person's being joyful, talented, abundant, or confident doesn't threaten another's ability to claim the same. The true concern is around the energy of arrogance. Arrogance is a defense mechanism of the ego. When people are coming from the fear paradigm, they are operating from the idea of hierarchy. To one degree or another, most of us have been deeply indoctrinated in this limiting belief. We must be very careful to not use our successes to belittle others or falsely make ourselves feel superior.

Just as I love to see my own children lit up with joy and confidence, engaged with life to the fullest, I believe God rejoices when we are in a state of hearty morale.

Our authentic empowerment will not be embraced by everyone around us, but illuminating what is possible for humanity is important sacred work. Seeing others thriving and shining raises the collective morale of all.

THE SYMPHONY

While the idea of infinite personal potential may be appealing on some level, I don't believe it's either true or desirable. I believe we are born with an essential shape, a form, and a function. Life adores variety and contrast.

Think of a musical instrument—a violin, piano, or set of drums. Each has a unique form and function. Each produces a unique sound, possesses specific qualities, has a specific method of being played, and is honored with its own place in the symphony. Your essential self is something to work with and care for in a similar fashion, something to discover and master.

A piano is a thing of beauty and expressive potential. It is an instrument with tremendous range, capable of playing high and low notes and minor and major chords and transitioning between the two in an instant. Imagine if we could view our own emotional range with the same respect. We would not take a hammer to the low notes of the piano and imagine that we had improved it.

Musicians care for and respect their instruments. They accept the limitations, physical reality, and boundaries of their instruments. Simply, being an oboe is different from being a guitar or a flute. Each requires unique care. You are an entity as distinct as an instrument. I believe that you have been formed by heaven's hands. The less energy you waste on attacking, abusing, neglecting, or judging your instrument, the better. It is always the mastery of your instrument and the playing of music that is your work. The instrument is sacred.

What possible use is there in judging or attacking your instrument? This is not modesty or humility; it is simply self-abuse. Honor your instrument. Honor your nature, your voice, and your physical self. Enjoy your own authentic expression. There is a place for you in the grand symphony. In fact, there is a need for what only you can express.

Where does your instrument end and your music, your practice, begin? This is a productive question. What do mastery and empowerment look like for you? As you release the struggle to be something other than what you are, you can apply the enormous return of focus and energy in more meaningful ways.

When we have truly come to respect and care for our instruments, we cannot help but respect the place of the other instruments. Without the drama of judging and comparing, we are left with awe and wonder at the wholeness of the symphony.

I do not believe in rejecting any part of self because when the whole is remembered, integrity is restored, and vigorous health is the result. The whole, vigorously healthy self is a joy to itself and an active participant in the healing of the whole of humanity and beyond.

There may be fear in claiming what you are because it also is saying what you are not. Will it be enough? Clarity comes from giving up inauthentic parts of yourself. Declaring your scope and therefore your limitations takes courage. As you "follow your bliss," as Joseph Campbell would say, you will develop your authentic gifts. With time, you find yourself more and more engaged with the activities that bring you joy.

The leap of faith required to imagine that what you most enjoy is your purpose is of paradigm-shift proportions. The idea that spending my time reflecting on the most delicious bits of spiritual inspiration I can find, inhabiting a world of beautiful words and imagery while composing and singing songs is a valuable use of time literally brings tears to my eyes.

Moving from guiltily squeezing these pursuits into my life to designing my entire life around these natural joys provides a relief I cannot name. The fact that I am ready to commit to my art is aligning me with the energy, joy, and discipline I have craved my entire life.

> "Your vocation in life comes from where your greatest joy meets the world's greatest need."
>
> —FREDERICK BUCHNER

CIVILITY

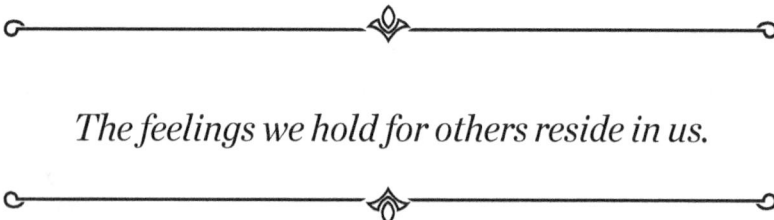

The feelings we hold for others reside in us.

Civility is the practice of bringing love to our relationships with others. I do not believe it is possible to truly honor the sacred within oneself without honoring the sacredness that is inherent in all of humanity. Civility is the means by which we practice, demonstrate, and honor the sacredness of life.

Can you imagine if we trusted and respected the individuals comprising the great, global human organism the way the human body trusts its cells? Every cell is encoded with a supportive role in the functioning of the whole. When individual cells are supported and receive the nutrients they require, they naturally serve, in their own unique ways, the needs of the whole.

I understand how insanely naive this sounds. Yet there is great wisdom for humanity in this metaphor. I wouldn't have the courage to write it if not for the clarity gained from personal experience. Trusting the intelligence behind my own unfolding allows me to see the innocence in both myself and all of humanity. Imagine a world in which every individual is encouraged to claim worthiness for themselves. This would create an enormous shift in collective energy from grand vicious cycles into grand virtuous cycles.

When we want to enter another's tender heart space, we must bring respect and safety. We must hold a safe place for buried beliefs and forgotten feelings to come into the light. As soon as we judge, defenses rise. Meaningful conversation and the chance for healing close. We must be aware of our goals. Are we aiming to judge or to heal? If you only want to judge or enrage another human being, that requires very little skill. You can slam a door in an instant, but what comes next? The skill of building bridges requires intention and focus with love.

We cannot expect to be heard if we do not listen.

In an episode of *Oprah's Master Class,* Diane Sawyer revealed that she believes all criticism is about making a request. "Why not just make the request instead?" The wisdom contained within this sentence is the ultimate drama buster.

When understanding and evaluating a situation, we must determine what we would like to create and what is within our power now to move reality in our desired direction. All drama serves only to delay action and deplete our resources. With love in our seat of personal power, we understand that acting with civility, clarity, and intention is the most rational, effective, and efficient path forward. Recognizing and honoring the power of others means we must act with civility in order to respond in solidarity.

One gift of the higher consciousness of humanity is our understanding of interconnectedness. The act of contributing to a cause reinforces the comforting belief that we are indeed part of something grander—a group that is organized under a common cause and mobilizing resources with the intention of preserving or problem-solving.

I was fascinated to discover a relatively recent cultural bias of distrust for institutions when I read *The Road to Character* by David Brooks. It is very sad to me that we have lost faith in institutions and the leaders of our times. Institutions can carry ideals in culture and society across generations and through difficult times when individual motivation for good might sag. For instance, an institution might concern itself with meeting the needs of the homeless 365 days a year rather than the waxing and waning concern most individuals experience based on season, state of economy, and significant holidays.

I believe we need robust institutions serving as long-term embodiments of living ideals in society. The corrosion of trust has not been without cause, but I believe the exposure of violations of trust can serve as evidence that checks and balances are in place and functioning effectively.

Importantly, trauma, violence, and the denial of the dignity of humanity must end. These offenses serve only to strengthen and extend vicious cycles into the future. This is true on societal and individual levels. Every individual who experiences the violation of fundamental rights and those who care for them will naturally carry forth fear and blame. The healing of wounds and injustices requires time and essential resources. The clearest, most effective and efficient path forward must be sought to transition from vicious to virtuous cycles.

I think about what I can personally do to heal distrust and cynicism. I try to live in my highest integrity while holding space for faith in positive change. The existence of corruption cannot serve as an excuse to ignore our hero's call. Each and every individual living from a higher standard of conduct elevates the whole of society. Inspiration is like light; it overcomes darkness by its very presence.

True love and innocence are not stingy; they are unlimited and eternal. The desire to limit salvation to a small group is a function of fear. It stems directly from a belief in scarcity. If we find that we wish to limit innocence, power, or abundance to ourselves or a group to which we belong, that is simply fear. The voice of fear can be recognized and released. By generously wishing for the highest good of all, we elevate all of mankind. We return dignity to the heart of human experience.

FROM ARCHETYPE TO EMBODIMENT

When I first began to play with the idea of becoming a songwriter, I was drawn to the stories of other songwriters. In the beautiful age of the podcast, finding interviews with songwriters sharing their own journeys is not difficult. One day I found a podcast called *Sodajerker On Songwriting* and listened to two interviews back-to-back: Hosier and Adam Duritz. During those two hours, the way I saw myself changed, and as a result, my personal mythology expanded. I knew with absolute confidence that I was a songwriter.

That is not to say I compare my talent or artistic style with theirs. Nor do I feel destined for or entitled to the type of success that they have known. I simply recognized myself in the stories they told about music and songwriting.

Adam Duritz shared the story of the first time he sat down at a piano to work out the chords of a song he had written. I was inspired to do the same.

I recognized the way inspiration came to me as part of my own artistic process. The way I scribbled lyrics on pieces of paper and pulled over in my car to capture melodies that floated through my mind—seemingly of their own accord.

I began to understand how the amorphous and impersonal archetype of the artist expressed itself personally in the individual artist. Hosier and Adam Duritz revealed to me the interior experience of the artist, complete with their own sense of limitations. They revealed how they overcome self-doubt and how they work with other artists, managers, and producers to create music. I understood I don't have to be good at *everything* to be a singer-songwriter.

The truth is, empowerment is always married to vulnerability and interdependence. When others honestly share their inner experiences, they let us know that the painful, uncomfortable, and messy feelings that come along with their journeys are part of the process. Experiencing these feelings does not mean we are lost or on the wrong path.

For the first time, I came to my art from a state of worthiness, not in an attempt to earn worthiness. I chose to honor the sacred calling to songwriting by pouring my essential resources into my art. I spent my time and focus working on lyrics and melodies. Finally, after decades of moving my beloved piano across the country, I sat down and started to play. I was inspired and in love with the process and began to engage with my sacred work. I was learning to embody my inner artist.

BECOMING VIOLETTA

When we desire to create something new, the first essential condition is space. Space to see what is not yet there and allow it to come into being. When we are so completely immersed in what we are "being," imagining the real possibility of being something new is quite difficult.

Violetta Jean is my professional name, not my real name. Violetta began as a personal exercise of imagination. What if I were completely and utterly free of all the stories of the past? No guilt, no path before me deemed impossible, too difficult, or too special for me. What if I considered myself worthy of anything I wished to create—my temperament, passions, interests, talents, and the wisdom of my years all fully possessed? Me, my full essential self, in a state of pure potential. My body, mind, spirit, and heart held in innocence.

I named this imaginary version of myself Violetta. If I hadn't decided that I was poor, invisible, and afraid, what might I be? If the simple fact that music and singing brought me tremendous joy was not questioned but fully embraced, what would I do? Would I wait to be chosen or choose for myself?

Violetta is my innocent essential self. She is a container of pure, unconditional love. The kind of love that I am striving to give my children. The kind of love I wish for you. In Violetta's love, my initial attempts at songwriting were praised! The quality of my songs or how green I was didn't matter. She was filled with joy and pride at every act of courage.

In Violetta, all my beautiful intentions burn bright and true. Violetta wishes for my genuine joy and happiness, not just productivity. Violetta sees clearly that my mistakes do not diminish me. She wishes to support and encourage my essential nature. Whether the gap between Violetta and what feels like me is wide or small, this I know: the only thing I want to fill that gap with is love.

Seeing truly in love, aligning in love, and acting from love is the path to all I seek. Love is the field of pure potential. My trust in love is complete. It is big enough to hold and carry doubt and fear.

Violetta was there when I sang and recorded my own songs, a cappella on my bathroom floor in a shaky voice. She was there when I found the courage to send them to a professional songwriting coach for the first time. She comforted me when the voice of my inner critic responded, *Oh, my God. What are you doing? Humiliating. He is going to be so disgusted he is not even going to know what to say. You are really putting him in a terrible position. So unkind.* Violetta feels the waves of nausea, shame, and doubt, but she is proud. *Look what you are doing! This is so brave. You are living the life you are meant for!*

How fascinating that I imagine that I am "making up" that I am a writer or a songwriter/singer, when that is, in fact, what I am drawn to do. It's what I am doing. Does a songbird need to pass a worthiness test, a talent competition, to sing? Violetta holds me in safety and demonstrates freedom. She is patient and kind.

I have chosen Violetta as my professional name for several reasons, the most important of which is that I want all of my work to carry the beautiful, sweet energy of unconditional love. My intention is for all my sacred work to come from my full, authentic, essential self.

It takes courage to carry vulnerability. Wisdom to hold ignorance, shame, and regret with dignity and compassion. Standing tall in the full glory of humanness requires more strength than my ego alone possesses. It requires the eternal, unconditional love of the Divine. Violet is the color of the crown chakra, connecting us to the Divine throughout our lives.

Pursuing my dreams also requires the sustaining, earthy, nourishing, joie de vivre of my soul. The holy place where all these meet is in my heart. This place is the only true and authentic source of my essential self, my love, my life, my art. This is where I find the morale of a songbird.

LIVING THE LIFE WE ARE CREATING

What most captures my heart about morale is the idea that we are always living with dignity and joy. Morale honors the fact that while we are always engaged in sacred work, never truly knowing what we may face in the future, we are *living* now.

Have you ever been swept away by the idea of creating something beautiful for yourself or your family? Perhaps the perfect back porch setting of comfort and beauty. An open invitation to rest, visit, and nourish the soul. The pillows set on the porch swing, the hammock gently swaying in the breeze. After its creation, how often have you actually laid down your work to savor the sweetness of this setting? How often do you actually enjoy the fruits of your labor? What fruits are available to savor in this season?

We can find beauty in every season when we are seeking it. Mother Nature's great show is indeed magnificent to behold. Maybe seasons keep changing to call our attention to them, call us back into the abundant now.

Look back fondly on the past, plan joyfully for the future, but mostly be present to the life before you now. Have faith that you will continue to reside in love for all the days of your life. You are the powerful cocreator of the feast before you now. The feast is present whenever you are willing to see it. May the feast last for all the days of your precious life.

SECTION VI
morale of a songbird - the album

THERE IS A BIRD THAT LIVES WITHIN MY HEART. HER sweet song carries joy, faith, and beauty from another realm. Her song is divine love. For most of my life, I have tried to protect this little bird, hiding her in a secret cage. It did not feel safe to free her in this world. But the truth is the innocence and love she holds are more powerful than any fear I've known.

Part of my sacred work has been to free my little bird and bring her song to the world. It has not been easy, and I have known fear, doubt, and despair. Still, my little bird has never left me.

Birds

Beauty's in the Dance

I Love You (my first song)

My Mythology

It's Not Christmas

Deciduous

Clichés

To Not Love Well

Cinderella Soul

The Sun

Doldrums

Heroine

Constellations

Old Time Gospel Song (Ode to Shug Avery)

Little Flower

Old Bulova

La Reine est sur le Trône

BIRDS

Just another girl,

Singin' out her heart,

What's this old world

Gonna do with me?

Then I think about the birds

Singin' on a branch,

And they don't worry

'Bout things like that.

Just as the birds above,

I was born of Heaven's love.

They don't question their colors.

They join the Heavenly chorus,

And they sing,

And they sing.

You know a weary bird

By its sorrow song.

I couldn't sing a word,

Afraid to get it wrong.

Now I think about the birds

Singin' on the branch,

And I don't worry

'Bout things like that.

Just as the birds above,

I was born of Heaven's love.

They don't question their colors.

They join the Heavenly chorus,

And they sing,

And they sing.

Oooh, it's time

To move on down the line.

Remember, I've always held the key

To this cage.

There's no need to be afraid,

Lost in doubt and shame.

This simple truth remains.

Just as the birds above,

We are born of Heaven's love.

They don't question their colors.

They join the Heavenly chorus,

And they sing,

And they sing.

I'm ready to sing.

BEAUTY'S IN THE DANCE

Maybe it's a sin,

Always trying to transcend.

We only have this little while

To be human.

The Earth, the Divine,

Are forever intertwined.

The sun is king, the earth his queen.

Their dance is time.

La Grande Beauté, La Grande Souffrance,

The Beauty's in the dance.

Sweet Trinity in harmony,

We never know how long.

Moving to the melody

Of love's eternal song.

You know I love romance,

But the Beauty's in the dance.

The curtains are drawn.

It's a Masquerade Ball.

Recall your invitation Dear,

Before they fall.

Reality and dreams,

More connected than they seem.

Our partner in the dance remains

A mystery.

La Grande Beauté, La Grande Souffrance,

The Beauty's in the dance.

Sweet Trinity in harmony,

We never know how long.

Moving to the melody

Of love's eternal song.

You know I love romance,

But the Beauty's in the dance.

Together then apart,

It's the subject of all art.

Yet nothing's lost, all still resides

Within your heart.

Poetry and prose,

Of love they are composed.

Beware the thorn, but don't forget to

Pluck the rose.

La Grande Beauté, La Grande Souffrance,

The Beauty's in the dance.

Sweet Trinity in harmony,

We never know how long.

Moving to the melody

Of love's eternal song.

You know I love romance,

But the Beauty's in the dance.

I LOVE YOU

(My first song, written when I was six or seven)

I love you.

I love you.

The most I can do

Is love you,

And love you I can do.

I trust you.

I trust you.

The most I can do

Is trust you,

And trust you I can do.

I thank you.

I thank you.

The most I can do

Is thank you,

And thank you I can do.

And trust you I can do.

And love you I can do.

MY MYTHOLOGY

Born of May in Flora's State,

Scottish blood warmed by southern sun.

My mom says I came out fae,

Well I guess that's okay.

True colors light the way.

And so began my mythology.

Immortal love born in family,

The home of gold and alchemy.

Childhood held in sense and memory,

Rich in love and imagery.

I carry you in my mythology.

She's never known a setting sun.

Rightly named for song of joy.

My mom showed us life is fun.

Each day's a blessing, every one.

Her light is boundless love.

And so began my mythology.

Immortal love born in family,

The home of gold and alchemy.

Childhood held in sense and memory,

Rich in love and imagery.

I carry you in my mythology.

His Corduroy voice and Oklahoma Hills,

The soundtrack of my childhood made.

Dad's oil paints my senses filled.

His kind and twinkling eyes reveal,

The magic of a boyhood still.

And so began my mythology.

Immortal love born in family,

The home of gold and alchemy.

Childhood held in sense and memory,

Rich in love and imagery.

I carry you in my mythology.

A carefree son of hot July,

Daniel recalls the fondest times.

The two of us were born in tune.

My brother through and through,

As faithful as the moon.

And so began my mythology.

Immortal love born in family,

The home of gold and alchemy.

Childhood held in sense and memory,

Rich in love and imagery.

I carry you in my mythology.

IT'S NOT CHRISTMAS

It's not Christmastime,

But carols of old are on my mind.

For old words, like old friends hold,

Comfort for the soul.

And I know that it's not Christmas,

But is it too much to ask?

Comfort, joy and hope to last

The whole year through.

On this ordinary night,

Holy light shines just as bright.

Revealing beauty far and near

In all that we hold dear.

The world in fear falls to despair.

But for the grace of Mother Mary,

A baby wrapped in loving arms,

Is safe from worldly harm.

And I know that it's not Christmas,

But is it too much to ask?

Comfort, joy and hope to last

The whole year through.

While we pray for peace on earth,

And the soul to feel its worth.

Angelic voices can be heard

The whole year through.

By whatever name you call the star

That brightens winter's darkest hours.

Its light is love, it burns in us.

This we all can trust.

And I know that it's not Christmas,

But is it too much to ask?

Comfort, joy and hope to last

The whole year through.

While we pray for peace on earth,

And the soul to feel its worth.

Angelic voices can be heard

The whole year through.

It's not Christmastime,

But carols of old are on my mind.

For old words, like old friends, hold

Comfort for the soul.

DECIDUOUS

Summer's leaves begin to fall,

Sweet Persephone's recalled.

Southern birds in flight

Leave me feeling small.

Alone in an empty room,

My muse has flown the coop.

Let go, there's nothing else to do.

I've always been deciduous.

By now I've come to trust

Life flows through the barren branch.

Just as love flows to the broken heart

And makes it whole.

Oh, there's Beauty in deciduous.

Winter's darkness starts to grow.

Cold wind howls and bites the bone.

Time to tend the flame within.

Yet Church bells still do toll.

For winter's grace is faith.

Cherry blossoms in the vase,

With meager hope and cheer I wait.

I've always been deciduous.

By now I've come to trust

Life flows through the barren branch.

Just as love flows to the broken heart

And makes it whole.

Oh, there's beauty in deciduous.

Spring calls home the joyous lark,

Warms Persephone's dear heart.

Leaves reborn in green.

Perfume floats through screens.

My faith has been renewed.

The sky's the fairest blue.

I sing a song to please my muse.

I've always been deciduous.

By now I've come to trust

Life flows through the barren branch.

Just as love flows to the broken heart

And makes it whole.

Oh, there's beauty in deciduous.

Summer days grow long,

There's been beauty all along.

Branches bow in gratitude.

Sweet hours spent with my muse.

Birds praise in serenade,

Before the bounty fades,

Enjoy the feast our Mother's made.

CLICHÉS

Thank you for coming to the door.

You'd rather be left on your own, I know.

No need to pretend any more.

There's no place I'd rather be.

I know this isn't pretty, little pain,

Turned bittersweet in melody. (so)

I won't give you any clichés.

I won't tell you that it's all okay. (Not today)

I'll just sit with you in silence

And surround you with my love.

When morning comes there's still no joy.

It's hard to carry all the weight these days.

Can't name the sorrow your heart holds.

No need to argue with the night.

When darkness falls, lay down the fight and rest.

It takes too much to hold so tight.

I won't give you any clichés.

I won't tell you that it's all okay. (Not today)

I'll just sit with you in silence

And surround you with my love.

Despair is hard to bear alone.

Even while it makes you want to hide

From pain as heavy as a stone.

When there's no cushion to the bone.

Just let me be the comfort that you need.

So you can feel you're not alone.

I won't give you any clichés.

I won't tell you that it's all okay. (Not today)

I'll just sit with you in silence

And surround you with my love.

(Outro)

Take the time it takes, dear.

I'm here to love you all the way.

TO NOT LOVE WELL

You and I both know

We are bound for heaven's gate.

We may as well turn to face

Each other now.

Because it hurts to not love well.

Aw, it hurts to not love well.

Brother sister, mother child,

Friend to friend & foe to foe.

Yes, and lovers too.

Precious time is flowing by,

Don't want to wait til all is lost.

To thaw the winter frost,

Give up this fight.

How can so much tender love

Turn into angry words?

Each one regretted afterwards.

Let's rise above.

Because it hurts to not love well.

Aw, it hurts to not love well.

Brother sister, mother child,

Friend to friend & foe to foe.

Yes, and lovers too.

Who is heard if no one listens?

We only judge, not understand.

Why make a stand

If no one wins?

I make a vow, I won't compare

Your precious real to my ideal.

On this I place a seal,

The love we share.

Because it hurts to not love well.

Aw, it hurts to not love well.

Brother sister, mother child,

Friend to friend & foe to foe.

Yes, and lovers too.

You and I have known

A love cowritten by the Fates.

With fortunes shared, we come to face

That we are one.

Because it hurts to not love well.

Aw, it hurts to not love well.

Brother sister, mother child,

Friend to friend & foe to foe.

Yes, and lovers too.

(Outro)

You are my Love, that's all I know.

So meet me at the kitchen table,

Defenses down, as we are able.

We'll find a way

To love each other well.

CINDERELLA SOUL

Hold courage in your heart my Dear.

Cry until your ancient tears run clear,

And they will turn to tears of joy.

Climb the winding attic stairs with grace.

Let woes pass by and leave no trace.

Truth is only seen in innocence.

Shine the light and darkness goes.

The Queen cannot be overthrown.

Beauty in the garden grows

Behind the iron gate.

Sing a joyful song of faith.

Reveal your Cinderella soul.

Remember gentle is invincible.

Your greatest strength's invisible.

In noble sweetness smile the while.

Tend these earthen fields of soil,

And they will turn to fields of gold.

True home is found in destiny.

Shine the light and darkness goes.

The Queen cannot be overthrown.

Beauty in the garden grows

Behind the iron gate.

Sing a joyful song of faith.

Reveal your Cinderella soul.

We know just how the story goes.

Carry on, your path foretold.

Your happy ever after waits.

Shine the light and darkness goes.

The Queen cannot be overthrown.

Beauty in the garden grows

Behind the iron gate.

Sing a joyful song of faith.

Reveal your Cinderella soul.

THE SUN

As I lay on the kitchen rug,

Bathed in the morning light,

I could feel through the window,

And the cold winter snow in flight,

Across the blue mantle of Mary,

Hung in the morning sky,

The warm rays of our dear sun,

Straight through darkness, space, and time,

As if we were in the same room.

And that is when I knew,

That your love will always find me,

And my love will always reach you.

DOLDRUMS

I'm living how I want,

But I don't want much.

Feels like there's not enough

Of something I've got to hold on to.

Which word best describes

The empty pit in me?

Despair, ennui or melancholy?

Doesn't really matter, a hole's a hole.

What can be done

When doldrums come?

I've lost my muse,

Can't bear the news.

I've come undone.

The wine just numbs.

It's just no fun

When doldrums come.

On days like today

I don't like my voice.

The world is full of empty noise.

My melody falls flat and tired.

Oh God, I hate the way

Road kill makes me feel.

Irreverence for life is all too real.

Such waste tears the tender heart in two.

What can be done

When doldrums come?

I've lost my muse,

Can't bear the news.

I've come undone.

The wine just numbs.

It's just no fun

When doldrums come.

No happy endings come to mind.

All the colors drained,

My thoughts are just a sad refrain.

What's the use, I'll just go back to bed.

What can be done

When doldrums come?

I've lost my muse,

Can't bear the news.

I've come undone.

The wine just numbs.

It's just no fun

When doldrums come.

HEROINE

I wrote myself

Right out of my story

When I couldn't find

The heroine in me.

Now I'm calling, I'm calling

Won't you please come home to me?

Bring back your audacity.

Bring back your joie de vivre.

I've been like a bell without its ring,

Living this life without your song.

Somewhere between

The dreaming and sinning,

I really thought

I'd lost my innocence.

Through all my years

I've wandered far and wide.

Some days are hard,

I won't even try to lie. (So)

Now I'm calling, I'm calling

Won't you please come home to me?

Bring back your audacity.

Bring back your joie de vivre.

I've been like a bell without its ring,

Living this life without your song.

What can't be lost

Need never be found.

The tales of old will

Never keep me bound.

Now I'm calling, I'm calling

Won't you please come home to me?

Bring back your audacity.

Bring back your joie de vivre.

I've been like a bell without its ring,

Living this life without your song.

Lost at sea,

The siren song floats by...

You know I came

To know it, line by line.

Yet by and by

Sweet innocence returned

From deep within the heart

Of a little girl.

Not going to wind up a cautionary tale.

No, I'm writing a living fairy tale.

Bring back your audacity.

Bring back your joie de vivre.

I've been like a bell without its ring,

Living this life without your song.

(I swear Odysseus

Found the shorter way Home.)

(Outro)

Not going to wind up

A cautionary tale.

I'm the heroine

Of my own fairy tale.

CONSTELLATIONS

Tonight,

You hold the door for her.

I know your smile,

Your sweet flirtatious charm.

Your hands are soft and warm.

She is beautiful and kind.

Lovely as you'll ever find.

You've done nothing wrong

In trying to find your way.

Does she realign the stars?

I know I left you in the dark.

No amount of past can buy a present,

But what if you knew...

I didn't mean to grow so cold.

My heart turned in to guard its flame.

Love can burn beneath the known.

I wish that I could hold you now.

What makes us hide the love we've shown?

The truth be told,

I still don't know.

The night

We walked beneath the stars,

Your hand in mine.

We spoke of dreams for hours.

It seemed the world was ours.

The shifting constellations

Revealed our maps as one,

And I shone bright for you.

We took the vows in faith,

Blind to all we had to heal,

For day reveals what night conceals.

No amount of past can buy a present,

But what if you knew...

I didn't mean to grow so cold.

My heart turned in to guard its flame.

Love can burn beneath the known.

I wish that I could hold you now.

What makes us hide the love we've shown?

The truth be told,

I still don't know.

But I need you to know,

I still want you.

I don't want you to go,

Feeling you're not enough.

I'd proudly call you my man

For all the days of my life.

I didn't mean to grow so cold.

My heart turned in to guard its flame.

Love can burn beneath the known.

I wish that I could hold you now.

What makes us hide the love we've shown?

Must be the fear

We're all alone.

So tell me now.

Promise I'll be okay.

Tonight, I'm praying for grace.

Are the very constellations

Shifting above your heads?

Or do I

Still shine bright

For you?

OLD TIME GOSPEL SONG (ODE TO SHUG AVERY)

I need an old time gospel song

To fill my soul.

I'm feeling low.

Oh you just don't know.

I need an old time gospel song

To carry on.

I've given my all.

Lord let me stand tall.

My weary heart needs something to beat to.

My hips need something to sway to.

My arms need something to raise to.

I need an old time gospel song.

I need an old time gospel song

To fill my soul.

I'm not alone on this boat,

And I sure wanna float.

I need an old time gospel song

To make my way.

Don't let these waves

Come and wash me away.

My weary heart needs something to beat to.

My hips need something to sway to.

My arms need something to raise to.

I need an old time gospel song.

Lord reach down

To where I am right now.

Oh I've been lost.

Lord, Let me be found.

My weary heart needs something to beat to.

My hips need something to sway to.

My arms need something to raise to.

I need an old time gospel song.

(outro)

Oh sweet Lord,

Gather me body and soul

And carry me home.

LITTLE FLOWER

Oh Little Flower,

When did you turn your face from the sun?

You can't even face the love in my eyes.

Shadows fall behind

When we just turn to face the sun.

My precious flower,

Turn your face to the sun.

In fear and shame we hide.

We feel unworthy of the light.

We turn to ease the pain.

As within, so without.

Holy light removes all doubt.

Turn your face to the sun.

Oh Little Flower,

When did you turn your face from the sun?

You can't even face the love in my eyes.

Shadows fall behind

When we just turn to face the sun.

My precious flower,

Turn your face to the sun.

Just as above, so below.

In love we're free to grow.

Turn your face to the sun.

Oh Little Flower,

When did you turn your face from the sun?

You can't even face the love in my eyes.

Shadows fall behind

When we just turn to face the sun.

My precious flower,

Turn your face to the sun.

In love and pride we shine.

We know we're worthy of the light.

We turn to heal the pain.

OLD BULOVA

I wanna wind up my days

In the old vintage way.

Sweet golden hours reclaimed for Love

On my old Bulova.

Everyday's a trinity,

Sacred work, play and dreams.

Hours to follow my muse, a few

To do just as I choose.

This little life of mine

Is sweeter than the finest wine.

I'm gonna keep my time

On an Old Bulova.

For peace of mind, I've got to find,

In all the hours as they unwind,

At least one hour that doesn't pull

On my old Bulova.

There's no need to rewind.

There's never been a better time.

Just wanna find some grace today,

Winding up my day.

This little life of mine

Is sweeter than the finest wine.

I'm gonna keep my time

On an Old Bulova.

The sun will rise, the sun will fall.

We mourn the passing of it all.

When heartstrings pull us ever home,

We find we're not alone.

This little life of mine

Is sweeter than the finest wine.

I'm gonna keep my time

On an Old Bulova.

At the end of the day,

I fold my hands and I pray.

To know the joy once more of

My old Bulova.

LA REINE EST SUR LE TRÔNE

(sung as chant)

Il y a une reine

Qui est assise,

Sur le trône d'or

Au centre de mon être.

Elle règne avec amour,

Son souffle porte la joie.

Sa langue est la beauté.

(Drop, dance rhythm begins)

I wear my past like a sweet perfume.

I'm only keeping what I love.

C'est le coeur de l'alchimie.

Now there's freedom in my body.

Honey on my tongue, oh.

La Reine est sur le trône, oh

La Reine est sur le trône.

Violet mysteries in my veins.

Life will never be the same.

La Reine est sur le trône.

Now my map holds four cardinals.

A golden compass in my hand.

(La douce liberté est à moi)

The jewels of my Queen's crown,

The only wealth I seek.

***La Reine est sur le trône,* oh**

La Reine est sur le trône.

Violet mysteries in my veins.

Life will never be the same.

La Reine est sur le trône.

All the stars

And the planets

In the black velvet

Sky

Whisper, dance.

Je ne peux pas chanter plus,

C'est trop beau pour les mots.

epilogue

THREE YEARS HAVE PASSED SINCE I BEGAN THE JOURNEY TO find the source of my morale. When I first began, I could not have imagined how long writing this book would take. Life follows a path more difficult and complex than any of us could ever predict. Along the way, our paths become entangled with the paths of others in our intimate circles and are sometimes altered entirely by the great coauthor.

Perhaps we would not choose to even begin the journey of personal transformation if we knew how grueling it would be. Yet I believe the veil of mystery is good. Life is infinitely more beautiful, exciting, and fulfilling because of the odysseys we choose to embark upon.

Some things have changed with the passing of time, and many things remain the same. The cats still get hairballs, housework gets backed up, and I still get irritable when I'm hungry and tired. I still dwell in the tension between my ego, soul, and higher self, and I am still engaged with *la grande beauté* and *la grande souffrance* of life. I am still human. I have not evolved past the messiness, stress, and difficulty of real life.

One thing has changed, though. I am no longer struggling to feel my own worthiness. Come what may of my music, this book, or any other goal I hold, I know that I am worthy of unconditional love. Somehow, messily, erratically, but with undying perseverance and faith, I have made the paradigm shift to love. I truly believe that the most powerful and efficient path to wholeness resides in love.

I no longer feel like there is a parallel, better life that I wish I was living. I no longer feel like there is some better version of myself living a life that I am too afraid to live. I am being and doing what I love. I am where I want to be and with the people who mean the most to me. I am home.

I no longer question if the Divine is present in my personal life, caring and communicating with me through the intimate details of my days. Faith is reaching for something unseen, not something that is unreal. I wrote this book for my children, in case I'm not around when they are in need. I would not encourage them to reach for something that is not real, something that is not there. The Divine is there, and its support is as real as whatever is supporting your physical body right now: the bed, the chair, the ground. The Divine is just as reliable, just as real.

As I conclude the process of writing this book and my first album of songs, I am finding the courage to put my sacred work out into the world one day at a time. As this creative phase comes to an end, I turn my attention to what I want to create next. I have gained trust in myself to navigate the unknown. I know I can manage the fear and anxiety that will surely accompany this next stage of my development as an artist.

I don't know what, if anything, will become of my creative work in the world. Old fears conquered have made room for the new fears before me now. I find as our lives unfold and we evolve, we trade one set of challenges for another. I don't know if I will ever overcome my fear of singing in front of people or if there is joy in performing for me. Yet I now trust myself to follow my heart and grow in a way that is true to my essential self. There is genuine joy in my days. I am more fulfilled now than at any other period of my life.

Now is enough, good enough, and soon enough.

acknowledgments

FIRSTLY, I WOULD LIKE TO THANK MY FAMILY. A BOOK IS A room within which an author must spend a great deal of time, focus, and energy. Thank you to my children for respecting my work and allowing me the time and space required to write this book. I would also like to express the utmost gratitude to my wonderful husband, Nick, who has supported me along every step of writing and publishing *Morale Matters*.

I would also like to thank my family of origin for a lifetime of love and support steeped in imagination. There truly is alchemical gold within the container of family. As my family has grown throughout the years, every member has added to the wealth and beauty of the whole.

I would like to thank the *entire* Scribe Media team for bringing this book to reality. Meghan McCracken, Emily Gindlesparger, Chas Hoppe, Hussein Albaiaty, Laura Call, Sophie May (the leader of my A Team), Anna Dorfman (the cover!), Ami Hendrickson, Tracy Hundley—all caring and gifted individuals. I feel blessed to have worked with each of you.

Thank you to my songwriting coach, Mark Cawley, for his extraordinary support and wisdom, and to Rick Ferriss for setting up my first recording studio.

I would like to acknowledge the following authors and spiritual leaders for decades of comfort and inspiration; you have shone a light through all of my darkest hours: Thomas Moore, Sarah Ban Breathnach, Teresa of Avila, Joseph Campbell, Marianne Williamson, Rumi, Khalil Gibran, Carolyn Myss, David Brooks, Carol S. Pearson, Gabby Bernstein, and Marie Forleo for the term multipassionate.

The following individuals were instrumental in helping me become empowered on a granular level. Thank you, Tonya Leigh, for sharing your own authentic path of personal growth with your community and keeping the process of "becoming" beautiful and fun. Thank you, Hilary Rushford, for sharing your own book journey and for the gift of Elegant Excellence. I would like to express my deep gratitude to April and Eric Perry at LearnDoBecome, and Amy McCready for creating Positive Parenting Solutions®.

To all the singer-songwriters and musicians, thank you for filling my life with music! As long as humanity carries on, there will be fresh music to express its heart and soul. Particular thanks to Dolly Parton, Ashley Monroe, Emmylou Harris, Sarah McLachlan, David Gray, Otis Redding, Aretha Franklin, Tata Vega as the immortal Shug Avery, Kacey Musgraves, the Beatles, Indila, Enya, Cyndi Lauper, Whitney Houston, Joy Williams, Maren Morris,

Alison Krauss, Dolores O' Riordan and the Cranberries, Khalid, Noah Cyrus, and Tori Amos.

Finally, because dance is communion with the Divine, a special thank you to Lady Gaga, Stromae, Marshmello, Lil Nas X, and Ellie Goulding.

about the author

VIOLETTA JEAN is a singer-songwriter, author, and former nurse devoted to creating works of comforting inspiration. She explores the human experience and our relationship with the mysterious Divine through the lenses of spirituality, psychology, science, religion, mythology, and art. She is a perpetual seeker of her core values of faith, beauty, and joy in the everyday. A wife and mother of three, she is currently savoring life on a coastal Maine farmette. You can find her at violettajean.com.

notes

NOTES

NOTES

MORALE MATTERS

www.ingramcontent.com/pod-product-compliance
Lightning Source LLC
Chambersburg PA
CBHW060514080526
44586CB00012B/483